Comfort and Protest

Also published by The Westminster Press

When Prayer Makes News
Edited by Allan A. Boesak and Charles Villa-Vicencio

Comfort and Protest
Reflections on the Apocalypse of John of Patmos

Allan A. Boesak

The Westminster Press
Philadelphia

Book design by Gene Harris

First edition

Published by The Westminster Press®
Philadelphia, Pennsylvania

PRINTED IN THE UNITED STATES OF AMERICA

9 8 7 6 5 4 3 2 1

Library of Congress Cataloging-in-Publication Data

Boesak, Allan Aubrey, 1946–
   Comfort and protest.

   Bibliography: p.
   1. Bible. N.T. Revelation—Criticism, interpretation, etc. 2. Government, Resistance to—Biblical teaching. 3. Church and state—South Africa—History—20th century. 4. Church and state—Biblical teaching. 5. South Africa—Politics and government—1978–   . 6. Boesak, Allan Aubrey, 1946–   .
I. Title.
BS2825.2.B64 1987   228'.06   86-28076
ISBN 0-664-24602-8 (pbk.)

For all those who, true to their faith, have struggled and fought with us; gone to jail and shared pain and bread with us. They are seeing the power of the beast. They shall see the victory of the Lamb.

Also dedicated to Paul Louis Lehmann on the eightieth anniversary of his birth, 10 September 1986

To be sure, if the Lord has called us to this battle, in vain have you kept such a vigilant, attentive watch for so many nights and days. The will of Christ will be fulfilled. For Jesus is our omnipotent Lord: this is our faith. What he commands will be done. It is not right for us to oppose the divine will. . . . But in the prince's council, Christ is not a guilty defendant, but a judge.

—Ambrose of Milan

Hitler has shown himself clearly for what he is, and the church ought to realize with whom it has to reckon.

—Dietrich Bonhoeffer of Germany

Mr Minister, you are not God. You are merely a man. And one day your name will only be a faint scribble on the pages of history while the name of Jesus Christ, the Lord of the church, lives forever.

—Desmond Tutu of Soweto

Contents

Foreword

When Allan Boesak was in solitary confinement in a Pretoria, South Africa, prison in the summer of 1985 he experienced what he called an "angelic visitation." As for the prisoner on the island of Patmos, so for Boesak; both the "comfort and the protest" of the Lord became dramatically real to him. He felt neither alone nor in fear of the "beast" that threatened his life. His confidence was deepened and his power to protest strengthened. In the moment when his life was in peril, he knew the power of true living as a divine gift. The angels confirmed it.

Allan had been reading Eberhard Bethge's book on Dietrich Bonhoeffer. He noted that Bonhoeffer had asserted not only that there are some things for which one *ought* to die but that there are some things for which one *must* die. Life rests in ultimate commitment. Hours of meditation on that fact yielded both conviction and deep assurance and peace. The dark prison cell became a center of illumination. "Comfort and protest" are grounded in the source of life itself—the One in whom "we live and move and have our being."

Before his arrest, Allan had been working on the manuscript for this book. In fact, he had been probing the meaning of the Apocalypse of John for several years and had both lectured and preached on certain passages on various occasions.

During those same years he had become a world figure.

Already a critical voice in and beyond the church in South Africa, in a few short years he became a crucial voice on the world scene in both religious and secular circles.

Ten years ago he published *Farewell to Innocence,* a devastating theological critique of apartheid which destroyed the ideological base of that inhumane system. His writings have now appeared in nine languages and are widely read around the globe. His was the key voice in the move to declare apartheid heresy, a judgment confirmed by the World Alliance of Reformed Churches in 1982 at its meeting in Ottawa, Canada. At that same meeting the Alliance elected Allan president of its organization of 70 million Protestants living on six continents.

He has been a most articulate theological voice not only for the millions in the Alliance but also and increasingly for Christians of all traditions who need his incisive expression of their faith, hope, and love. Few theologians, if any, are so much in demand by the people of faith in every land. Literally millions hear him gladly, not because of his "soothing words" but because of his prophetic protest in a world that worships comfort purchased with the blood of the oppressed. They hear in his speech not simply the voice of Boesak but the word of the Lord. They hear a faithful witness and rejoice.

His unflinching theological stance and the people's response to it, from his own local parish to the ends of the earth, have inevitably roused the interest of those in the political and social arena. Nadine Gordimer, the South African writer, once introduced Allan to a New York audience as "the young man who has taken a hand in history." So he has. What is more apparent to Allan is that history has taken a hand in his life. He once commented, "I no longer have a life of my own," to which anyone aware of his schedule can easily attest. Those who work at politics, those trying to shape public and common life, are anxious to set his agenda and if possible co-opt his voice. They are both fascinated and challenged by the meeting of theology and political reality in his mind. It is a powerful phenomenon foreign to many who would play cheap politics in our

time. Why a speech by him should be able to call forth so
powerful a movement as the United Democratic Front, a
leading resistance movement in South Africa, is a fascinating mystery, if not also an immediate political threat or
promise. Our secular age is forced to ask, "What is going
on here?"

When Boesak reflects critically on so tantalizing a book
as the Apocalypse of John, neither the ideological dreaming of political power brokers, nor the fanatical fantasies
of *The Late Great Planet Earth,* nor the numerological
speculation of fundamentalist schemers, nor even the
technical minutiae of scholars determine his reading. As a
prisoner for Jesus Christ, a fellow disciple with John of
Patmos, and under the same pressure of the power of
imperial politics wedded to religion, he reads the writing
of a fellow pilgrim on the way of protest. The bright light
of the coming kingdom does not permit him to do otherwise.

"We have another Martin," commented several black
leaders after hearing Boesak speak recently in Washington, D.C. Boesak and King share a prophetic and apocalyptic vision with John of Patmos because they have all
known the reality of imperious oppression. Another John
of Patmos, another Martin Luther King! All who are
tempted to worship simple power concentration as the
adequate assurance of security would do well to think
again about how they read the Bible and the newspaper.
They can too easily misread the signs of the times.

Boesak, together with John of Patmos, might yet be
heard in time "to comfort the afflicted and afflict the comfortable" so that all of us may begin to live by the future
promised in Jesus Christ. For the future promised in the
nightmarish dreaming of purveyors of Armageddon theology or Star Wars or "evil empire" self-righteousness or
America First idolatry is too dark and grim for anyone to
live by. We need the confirmed vision from the dark cell
in Patmos, or Birmingham, Alabama, or Pretoria. Millions
"who have the eyes to see or the ears to hear" will rejoice
and not allow their comfort to silence their protest or their

protest to rob them of their true comfort. To live peaceably while battling for justice demands that we know the future which offers life and power in the present. That future speaks in this book.

By this short commentary Boesak has offered the American scene and the world a great gift.

Edward Huenemann
*Director of Theology
in the Global Context Program*

Preface

The Bible is the most fascinating, exciting book in all the world. It speaks to me with a power that goes beyond anything I know. Somehow, however, the meaning of the last book of the Bible had always eluded me. The usual fascination with numbers and symbols and endless speculation in so many commentaries about the Revelation seemed boring. I could not understand the book's relevance for the situation in which South Africa's oppressed people find themselves. After all, I thought, our people are dying, our townships are burning—the Apocalypse is best left to the fanatics and the escapists, or to the academics of rich countries who have time for games of empty speculation. But I have since discovered other views of Revelation.

Comfort and Protest was conceived in 1980 as a series of Bible studies for my local church. It was the year of the student uprising in Cape Town, following on Soweto 1976. The school boycotts left hundreds dead, many wounds that would never heal, and questions about faith and God to which I had no answer. Somehow, I don't know why, I turned to the words of John of Patmos, and for the first time I began to understand. The power of his testimony forever changed my life.

Since then I have preached, marched, demonstrated. Half my ministry has become a confrontation with the South African government and its forces, in the pulpit and, because of that, in the streets. Arrested, threatened, imprisoned in solitary confinement, walking into rifles and machine guns, tear-gassed in churches, faced with horrors I had never dreamed of, seeing our children die on the streets, watching South Africa becoming less and less our mother and more and more our grave—during these turbulent years I have written this book as I found time, in bits and pieces. After I started writing, the first state of emergency was declared. As *Comfort and Protest* is finally born, this page is written during yet another state of emergency.

During these years, I believe, I have discovered the heart of that lonely, brave prophet on his island: with fear and trembling, yes, but also with a joy that no one can take away. For I know now what he knew then. Jesus Christ is Lord.

A.A.B.

Friday, 11 July,
in the Year of our Lord 1986
The 29th day of the state of emergency,
the 54th day after Pentecost

Introduction:
Underground Letters
to a Persecuted Church

The Revelation to John, as this book is known, is "apocalyptic literature." "Apocalypse" literally means "unveiling"—things that have been concealed become revealed, uncovered, open. This type of literature always appears against a background of persecution and suffering, during a transition from one period in history to another. It is always meant as comfort, encouragement, and inspiration for people in times of dire stress and great difficulties. It is mostly written in a language that can only be understood by those who share a common experience and a common faith.

As a type of literature, it appears to have been most prominent in the period between 200 BC and AD 200, four hundred years of crisis for Israel and the world. The Bible offers excellent examples of this kind of literature: Daniel (chs. 7–12), parts of the book of Ezekiel (chs. 38–39), Isaiah (chs. 24–27), and Zechariah (chs. 9–14). Examples of Jewish apocalyptic literature not included in the Bible are Judith, Baruch, Ezra, Enoch, and the Psalms of Solomon. Well-known sections from the Synoptic Gospels (see Matthew 24; Mark 13; Luke 21) also fall into this category, and then there is of course the apocalyptic work of the New Testament: the Apocalypse of John.

In these books the human figure is almost incidental, important only because it highlights the historical events and gives them human touchability, so to speak. What really matters here is the battle, the cosmic struggle between God and Satan, between the Creator and the great destroyer, between the Living One and the idol of death.

In the time in which John wrote the Apocalypse, there were other such writings by Jews who suffered likewise under the tyranny of Caesars. All these books seem to have much in common with apocalyptic literature in the Old Testament, but they were written pseudonymously, under the name of one or other respected and worthy figure in the history of Israel—Ezra, for example.

Written in the form of popular drama, mostly in Hebrew or Aramaic, these books were not only a reliving of historical events from ancient times but also sharp, critical commentary on contemporary historical events. The seer is engaged in long discussions with God. He prays, pleads, laments, while he is torn by anxiety and pain. The angel whom God sends to converse with him answers in a language clothed in mystery. The angel comforts him, admonishes, and gives advice. Finally, the angel also answers the many questions of the seer. In giving this reply, the angel reveals the secrets of history and of the future, allowing the seer to "see" what God has in mind for the future and for the history of humankind.

In the Apocalypse of John one finds all the classic elements of this type of literature: God in heaven, exalted far above the finiteness of human understanding, the angel descending to converse with the seer, the seer himself transported to the throne of God, the well-known symbols —child, woman, dragon, beast. Permeating all this mysterious language of signs and symbols and numbers and visions, and actually making it alive with meaning, are the deepest questions about human history, about God and Israel, and about the lot of God's people in the world, their pain, humiliation, and suffering. Here are the questions about the love and power of the living God, who remains God even though that love and power seem to disappear under the tidal wave of blind rage that the persecutor spews forth.

In these books Israel grapples seriously with the incomprehensible things of history: the destruction of Jerusalem and the temple, the exile, and the apparently uncontrollable might of the kings of the earth, who seem able to do with the people of God whatever they want. Here we are presented with the struggle to understand the meaning of history, the presence of God in the history of Israel, and the inexplicable chasm and relationship between God's promises and Israel's lot.

There is little doubt that this type of literature was a source of encouragement and hope to the entire Jewish people as they faced peril and threat at the hands of their enemies. In times of severe persecution, suffering, and death, the hearts of the faithful long passionately for signs of the power of God and for God's intervention in their history for the sake of justice and liberation. Apocalyptic works reflect in the most dramatic way the response of the people of God to the pressures of their time.

Such is the character of the Jewish books, the Apocalypse of Ezra and the Apocalypse of Baruch, written during the reign of the emperors Vespasian and Domitian. They could depend on a ready audience, because this type of literature had become an integral part of Israel's history of protest and because they had much in common with well-known books like Daniel.

Another characteristic of these books is their explicit political criticism. It should not really surprise us to hear from that great apologist of the Christian church Justin Martyr that in his time the reading and dissemination of Jewish apocalyptic literature was considered a crime under pain of punishment. Nor should it surprise us that during the Japanese occupation of Korea during the Second World War, Korean preachers were prohibited from preaching from Revelation.

For these reasons it is strange to find those who think that apocalyptic literature is really nothing more than "comfort through escapism," by which they mean that the explicit aim of the writer is to draw the attention of the people away from the harsh realities of their world by telling them how the seer is transported into another and

heavenly world through mysterious psychological experiences. Their attention is thereby focussed not on their
present plight and on ways to change that plight but on
the mysteries of God and on the future joys of a world yet
to come. So, for example, the angel says to Baruch, "Do not
be concerned about the fall of Jerusalem. Come, let me
show you the majesty of God." This is proof, so the argument goes, that for the apocalyptic writer the solution to
the problems of persecution and suffering lies in escaping
from this world into the dream world of the seer. Therefore, such critics say, what we find in a book like the
Apocalypse of John is nothing more than alienation from
this world and human history on a grand scale.

I do not find this argument convincing. Recent research
has shown that apocalyptic literature's primary concern is
precisely the situation in which God's people find themselves in this world, a situation that is caused by political,
social, and economic forces which are identified, challenged, and called to account in a unique way in this type
of literature. The writers of these books are as concerned
about the rebuilding of the just world as they are about the
destruction of the unjust world. Besides, central to all
apocalyptic literature is the figure of the political tyrant.
Characteristically, the tyrant is never called by his real
name, but the description of him is so accurate that there
can be little doubt as to his identity, once the time of
writing has been established and the political-historical
context is given its real weight. It is important to note that
the tyrant is always in competition with God. Indeed, he
sees himself as a god *in place of God,* and he expects from
his subjects the honour and submission one owes a god—
or, for the Jews and the Christians, God.

This is the way it is in the Apocalypse of John. He, like
the other writers of apocalyptic books, holds resolutely to
the certainty that the actions of political tyrants are essentially a challenge to the living God and a mockery of God's
name. They seem to have full control over this world and
God's people. But the faithful know that God cannot be
mocked; God's power cannot be challenged with impu-

nity, God's judgment will surely come upon those mighty and arrogant oppressors who like to play God in the lives of others.

Because of their political perception and challenge in such dangerous times, these books could not be written in the "normal" way. Any person who has ever lived under political oppression, where every move is watched and every word carefully weighed and where every other person could be an informer, knows this. Therefore these books were written in a way that only the initiated could really understand and draw encouragement from. These books were, in the real sense of the word, underground protest literature.

A Christian apocalypse

The Revelation to John is apocalyptic literature written for Jewish Christians in Asia Minor. However strange the language of John might sound to us today, for the readers in his congregations it was not strange at all—to the contrary. John's readers were acquainted with this kind of language and style from their own Jewish tradition, and John's liberal use of Old Testament material made understanding even easier. It is not only the visions and dreams which sound familiar. John sometimes takes symbols directly out of Old Testament apocalyptic material. Daniel's "one thousand two hundred and sixty days," for example, we find in Revelation 12:6; the characteristics of the beast from Revelation 13:2 are already known from Daniel 7. And of course John of Patmos has themes and style in common with writers of the extracanonical books like Ezra and Baruch, especially since they were written during the same period.

And yet there are a few remarkable differences between these books and the Apocalypse of John. To begin with, John, unlike the Jewish apocalyptic writers, does not use a pseudonym. In spite of the challenging and critical nature of his book, and in spite of the undeniable dangers that come with his preaching, he is quite open about his identity. Second, he does not build on events from ancient times. His theme is the immediate events of contemporary history. John speaks with an angel, but the one who lets him "see" is not an angel but the Lamb himself. John's revelation is not simply his own vision; he claims divine revelation. He opens with a sentence filled with authority: "The revelation of Jesus Christ . . . to his servant John."

Enemies of humanity

> To make a definite end to the speculations of the public, Nero decided to put the blame on those who were already hated by the people because of their shameful deeds, and he let them undergo the most refined ways of torture as punishment.
>
> The people called them Christians, a name derived from a certain Christ, who was executed by the procurator Pontius Pilate under Caesar Tiberius. Although suppressed for a short time, this pernicious foreign superstition reared its head again, not only in Judea, the cradle of this evil, but also in the capital city, where everything that is shameful and despicable comes together and proliferates. They have been arrested in the following way: first those who acknowledged readily that they were Christians, and then, at the indication of the prisoners, a great number of people. They were convicted, not so much because they were guilty of arson, but because of their hatred of all humanity.

This is the commentary of the Roman historian Tacitus on the events following the great fire which laid to ashes the greater part of the city of Rome in AD 64. These events were also the sign that the short and uneasy truce between the Christians and the Roman empire had ended. Very soon it became clear that what Rome really meant by the term "enemies of humanity" was "enemies of the state." What Rome wanted for itself was assumed to be also for the welfare of all humanity. Those who did not understand this, or questioned its logic, fell outside the bounds of consideration.

Christians had no place in Roman society. They could

never feel at home. They were persons of the third class. Romans, together with Greeks, belonged to the first class. On a very shaky second level were the Jews, and Christians were at the bottom of the ladder.

But again, what was meant by "hatred of all humanity"? And why was this the accusation against the Christians? Maybe we should say that the hatred, anger, and aggression directed against Christians was a result of Christian exclusivism and nonconformism. Roman society could not understand these people. They lived differently, talked differently, thought differently. And it was precisely this peculiarity, this uniqueness, this deviation from the accepted pattern which called forth the irritation—and especially the fear—that was the root of the enmity.

The expression "enemies of humanity" conveys the conviction of Roman society that Christians, because they refused to conform to the norms and rules of that society and because they, albeit quietly, said no to the existing social, political, and religious structures, were out to destroy these structures. Those who do not want to participate must have something else in mind. And there was a sense in which the Roman accusers had a point: The Christians *did* have something else in mind, which was indeed radically different from the Roman empire, and their rules of life could not square at all with the demands that emanated from Caesar's palace.

Of course Christians could not be accused of plotting the downfall of the emperor. Even less could they be accused of planning revolution. But no one, not the emperor and his political advisers or the so often fear-stricken church itself, could deny or avoid the political consequences of the gospel of the kingdom of God. And even though Christian apologists were emphatic that Christians were only normal persons, citizens who bore malice towards none, no one could deny the pious subversion that was inseparably linked to the confession to which these same Christians clung, tenaciously and resolutely—namely, Jesus Christ *alone* is Lord.

And because this confession had all kinds of conse-

quences for Christian attitudes toward politics, the emperor, military service, and so forth, Christians came to be
regarded more and more as a threat to the security of the
state and the welfare of its citizens. The fear of the total
collapse of the old, familiar structures in favour of a new
world order, the uncertainty caused by this small band of
people who persistently refused to deny their "mad superstition" even under the most horrific forms of torture—
these factors made it easy for Rome and its people to hold
Christians responsible for every conceivable setback and
disaster.

With more than a little bitterness, church father Tertullian wrote (and who can blame him for feeling bitter?), "If
the Tiber overflows its banks and threatens the city, if the
Nile refuses to overflow so that the land remains dry, if
there is an earthquake, or famine, or pest, the call is immediate: 'Feed the Christians to the lions!' "

All this was not only background to the Apocalypse of
John, it was the reality and indeed the experience of the
people for whom he wrote his letter. They were not super-
human beings, who through exceptional powers were capable of exceptional bravery. No, they were ordinary people, wary of informers and turncoats, certainly not looking
forward to the next round of torture, scared of those dark,
dank, stinking cells, scared also of the loneliness of dying.
But they passionately believed what had been proclaimed
to them: He who wants to hold on to his life at all costs shall
lose it. Whoever loses his life for my sake shall gain it. The
early Christians were no wild desperadoes or some kind of
Christian kamikazes who fanatically sought death. But
they had learned that *imitatio Christi* did not mean simply talking about Christ but following Christ, even unto
death. The report in Eusebius' *Ecclesiastical History* (4.
15) on the martyrdom of Bishop Polycarp puts it soberly:
"[We have] no praise for those brothers who give themselves up willingly to the authorities, but we do praise
those who work surreptitiously, go underground, and,
when they are caught, remain firm, even under suffering."

The Apocalypse of John is a letter of comfort to those

who, in the words of 1 John 1:1–2, have seen and are now witnesses. Augustine, in one of his sermons, translated this text as "We have seen and are now martyrs." In this way we can begin to see that the words of scripture are not meant to be read as beautiful and engaging prose, descending directly from heaven. They are, rather, words that come alive, find their shape, and are given birth out of the struggle with God for the sake of God and God's creation, a witness which is authenticated by God and in which the Spirit reveals God's life-giving power.

"Like Nero in his cruelty"

Questions about the authorship and time of writing of the Apocalypse of John have not been settled. Some think the emperor then must have been Caligula. Caligula was cruel enough to fit this role, and indeed we know he had tried to install an image of himself in the temple in Jerusalem. But Caligula died before he could enforce his divinity by law, and therefore much of what is said in the Apocalypse cannot be applied to him. Nero, however, remains a strong candidate.

Nero did indeed claim divinity, but he did not enforce its acceptance by the people. Although he was a tyrant and a persecutor of the church, it was apparently for reasons different from those we find in the Apocalypse, and the persecution he instigated probably remained confined to the city of Rome. Also, under Nero there seems to have been a measure of religious freedom, at least to the extent that in the beginning the Christians were able to proclaim their message quite openly. The Apocalypse is totally ignorant of such a period of relative rest and tolerance. The argument that the symbolic number 666 from Revelation 13 should be read as the numerical value of the name Nero is intriguing, but not convincing. (See chapter 5.)

Another possibility is that the Apocalypse was written during the reign of Caesar Domitian. This view seems to have the most merit for the following reasons. Domitian was the first Roman emperor to enforce his divinity by law. His cruelty was legendary; even academics who wish to pass a somewhat milder judgment on the man find themselves speaking about his "madness." Church father Tertullian speaks of him as "a second Nero in his cruelty." In other words, in him the church discovered a revived Nero, so much did this man's acts remind people of the ferocity of that first wave of oppression.

Domitian, the son of Vespasian, was enthroned in AD 81. He remained emperor until AD 96. He demanded that he be addressed as "My Lord and my God." Letters with his instructions began: "The Lord our God Domitian demands. . . ." We also know that he was adamant about being addressed by his divine title, *Deus et dominus noster Domitianus*—Our Lord and God Domitian.

The evidence we have from the early Christian church also corroborates the opinion that Domitian was emperor during the time John wrote the Apocalypse. The writings of church fathers such as Melito of Sardis, Irenaeus, Clement of Alexandria, Origen, and Victor of Rome, as well as the writings of that historian of the early Christian church Eusebius, all point to Domitian as the emperor under whose reign the Apocalypse of John was written. Irenaeus and Victor, especially, mention Domitian by name several times, and both say clearly (as does Eusebius) that John was banished to Patmos "for the sake of his faith in Jesus Christ and his witness before the world and the church" by Caesar Domitian.

It is accepted that at the centre of the Apocalypse lies the issue of obedience and loyalty—to God or to the deified Caesar. There was constant conflict between the claims of the emperor and what the church knew to be true. "To the churches in Asia Minor especially, Domitian's claim to divinity must have been a hard blow because the flourishing imperial cult in that region hardly permitted any avoidance of the conflict," writes historian Karl Baus (p. 132). "The pretext for the persecution in the eastern provinces was therefore based solely on the accusation of *lèse-majesté* which rejection of emperor worship involved."

So there are sound reasons for accepting that the Apocalypse of John was written during the time of Caesar Domitian and that the "beast" to whom John refers—that image par excellence of the earthly power who defies the Living God—was this Caesar, who, in his persecution of the church and in his nameless cruelty, was a reminder of the beasts the church had seen before: Antiochus Epiphanes, Nebuchadnezzar, and Nero.

Let me here make an observation about the ferocity of the debate on this particular point. The arguments around the different hypotheses seem to lead always to an effort to establish the truth by judging the *degree* of oppression that was meted out by one or another emperor. Whether it was Nero or Domitian or even Galba (as John A. T. Robinson suggests) is ultimately of secondary importance. To the suffering people of God it did not really matter who they suffered under. What mattered is that they suffered. In the same way it does not really matter that we do not know the precise identity of the Pharaoh of the exodus. But that God's people were in bondage—that mattered then as it matters now. We read history not in terms of relative differences between oppressors but in terms of the reality of suffering and oppression, the joys and the hopes of the little people of God. We see and understand the events of history from the underside. That perspective leaves little room for the academic consideration of differences that may have existed between Nero and Domitian, and it matters little that one may be described as "less oppressive" than the other. It is the fact that the weak and the destitute remained oppressed which provides the framework for understanding and interpreting history.

The Apocalypse of John

John himself was a Jewish Christian and in all probability a leader, possibly pastor to the churches of Asia Minor. His knowledge of the Old Testament, of Hebrew style and language, makes that evident. Exactly who this man was is not clear. John the apostle, the brother of Jesus, died a martyr's death before the Apocalypse was written. The grammar and style of the Johannine epistles are too different to have been written by the person who wrote the Apocalypse. The same is true for the Gospel of John. There is almost nothing in the Apocalypse to remind us of the Gospel of John. This causes most commentators to speak prudently of "John the Seer."

For us, the precise identity of the author of Revelation is not that important. There can be no doubt that he was someone with authority in the church in Asia Minor, a pastor who, according to his own testimony, struggled together with his church and suffered with his church for the sake of the gospel. His faith, obedience, and persistent discipleship brought him to the point where he had to choose: Domitian or Christ, the Caesar or the One who is Lord. He did not preach a disembodied gospel but, rather, felt the demands of this gospel in his own body, placing his own body, his own life, at risk for its sake. This discipleship inspired his church to remain faithful and caused the government to recognize in him an implacable foe. And it was this discipleship which caused Domitian to banish him to that forsaken island, Patmos.

There, John sees his visions of justice and love, of redemption and judgment. He sees what the emperor, in his blind arrogance, cannot see and what the people, in their fear and suffering, so easily forget: He sees life and sustenance for God's people. And from this island, around the year AD 95, John of Patmos writes his letters to the seven churches of Asia Minor.

From the very beginning John displays the strong influence of Old Testament thinking. Seven is a number suggesting completeness. The seven churches symbolize the *whole* church. By using this symbol, John not only passes beyond the borders of a specific geographic area, he also crosses the borders of his time and speaks to the church of Jesus Christ for as long as his voice can be heard. In so doing, he uses the language of the Old Testament. He reminds his readers of the history of Israel, drinking deeply from the wells of the stories about the exodus, the trek through the wilderness, and the promises of Yahweh that sustained the people throughout this history.

We must remember that during the century in which the texts of the New Testament were written there were no less than ten legal emperors. Some were gifted men who could afford to be somewhat tolerant; others behaved like madmen. Almost all were personally cruel and tyrannical and were involved in all kinds of atrocities. These people and the decisions they made had a marked influence on the young Christian church and on the writers of New Testament literature. Their deeds were seen and understood either as a blessing of God or rebellion against God. The ongoing struggle between the Caesar and Jesus Christ the Lord was decisive for the church. Nowhere is this struggle more pronounced than in the Apocalypse of John the Seer.

It is not true to say that the early Christians regarded the state as a "natural" enemy. For a while they reflected the very positive expectations scripture has of government. But at the same time it is true that they refused to let go of the confession that Jesus Christ, and he alone, is Lord. On this point, conflict between the interests of the state and the demands of the Word of God was both necessary and unavoidable. Both Jews and Christians persistently refused to acknowledge the divine status of the emperor. The result developed from discomfort and embarrassment in Rome to relentless persecution.

This conflict is the basic theme in the letter of John to the churches of Asia Minor. For, difficult as it was, the church was beginning to discover that the confession of Jesus the Messiah had consequences not only for the life of individual Christians and their church but also for the lives of nations and states. In an unambiguous way, John proclaims not just a personal ethic but the only true basis for a social and political ethic, the only true basis for a truly human world. The domain of the Lord and his people is not simply the world hereafter but the world here and now.

Those who have an ear

How should the message of John be understood? Three major ways of interpreting this book have been traditional and still are current today.

First of all, there is the so-called *preteristic interpretation,* which holds that the Apocalypse can be understood only in terms of the times in which the book was written. Because, in this view, the prophecies have all been fulfilled, the book has no relevance for today.

Second, there is the *futuristic interpretation:* everything of which John speaks is prophecy, and, as such, an "opening of the future," a perfect forecast of the end of times. For those who hold this view, ever since the book was written, every prophecy of John relating to the times between the writing of Revelation and the end time has come true, and we are now entering the final stage of history, also predicted accurately by the Apocalypse. All the prophecies will be fulfilled. This view is also called the "dispensationalist" view.

There is, third, the *continuing historical interpretation,* in which the Apocalypse is seen as picturing the progressive development of history. It shows a continuous thread running through the ages, from the time of John through the time of Constantine, the Protestant Reformation, to the time in which we now live, and into the future. As in the futurist interpretation, there is little concern for the historical context of the Apocalypse, and here as well there is an overwhelming emphasis on the symbolic language of the Apocalypse.

None of these interpretations is really satisfactory. Rather, a *contemporary-historical understanding* of the Apocalypse serves us best. John writes about the political situation in Asia Minor in his day and of the response of the church to that situation; his book cannot be understood outside of the political context of the time. But it is also prophecy. However, no prophecy receives its full and final fulfilment in one given historical moment only, or even in a series of events. If the prophecy is the expression of an undeniable truth which comes from God, it will be fulfilled at different times and in different ways in the history of the world.

This is the way in which the Revelation of John is to be understood. What was true in the time of John is proven to be true over and over again in the history of the church of Jesus Christ in the world. But the history of the world is not a different history from the history of the church. God calls the church which is in the world, and it is in this historical context that the church experiences the presence of this Lord, proclaims the message from this Lord, and erects signs of the kingdom of this Lord. Christians and the church are part of this history, not simply submerged by events that roll over them like waves from the sea. No, they are *in* history with responsibility *for* it—to challenge it, change it, undermine it, until it conforms to the norms of the kingdom of God and until the world recognizes the lordship of Jesus the Messiah.

At the same time, John points to the end and even anticipates and rejoices in the victory of the Lamb and the consummation of the kingdom. And this is why Revelation is so relevant for us today—not so much because we are intrigued by the symbolic language and the mysteries that abound in this book, nor because it is supposed to give us perfect forecasts of the hereafter—but because we see with some astonishment how truly, how authentically, that John, in describing his own time, is describing the times in which we live.

When we say the Apocalypse has a contemporary-historical meaning as well as being prophetic, we affirm the political message of this book. We begin to understand the reason behind the comfort and encouragement John wants to give the church. As with all apocalyptic literature, the direct reason for writing this book was the tension between the claims of the political tyrant and the demands of the God in whom the church believed, John's involvement, and the suffering of the church for the sake of the gospel.

"Apocalypse" for John thus meant God's final judgment

on the corrupt political and religious systems of oppression. Written in the secret language of apocalyptic writing, with symbols, numbers, and visions, it is a blistering criticism and a devastating judgment of Domitian and all autocrats like him who think they can challenge the Living One. This language was familiar to the Christians of Jewish descent who eagerly read this letter in their secret meetings.

For John and for the church, Domitian is without a doubt the instrument of Satan who persecutes the church, the power-mad fool who thinks he can be in competition with the God of heaven and earth, the idol who made himself into a god and who therefore, like all proud humans, will be "scattered in the imagination of his heart," "put down from his throne" by the One whose name is holy. The whole letter is a description of the battle between the Caesar who blasphemously claims divinity and the Lord, between Satan and the Messiah king. Chapter by chapter, almost verse for verse, Revelation is a polemic against the myths, legends, half-truths, and false pretenses which emanated from the imperial cult. Verse after verse also protests against the injustice, oppression, and persecution of God's people. Verse after verse offers comfort for this church under siege and assurance of the victory that belongs to the Messiah.

In a negative way, our point is made forcefully by New Testament scholar Robert Grant in *The Sword and the Cross*. Grant views Revelation as an overreaction to the too-zealous behaviour of a civil servant. For him the reason for John's banishment to Patmos was "not clear." John's Apocalypse is "full of hatred for Rome"; Grant is of the opinion that the richer churches of Asia Minor were far less enthusiastic about this book. This was also the reason why the Gospel of John was written, according to Grant, to make clear the true "otherworldly" nature of the Christian faith. In the Gospel of John it is accepted that the Roman state had divine authority and sanction and that Jesus' crucifixion was much more the result of the hatred of the Jews than of Rome. Here the Gospel is alien to and not involved with human affairs at all.

Reluctantly Grant concedes that the writer of the Apocalypse, in spite of the "subversive nature of his document," was right on one point: ultimately, there was no compromise possible between those who ceded all authority to the Roman state and those who believed that the state ought to be subjected to a higher authority: namely, that of God. Grant accuses the writer of the Apocalypse of "exaggeration, dreaming, and hatred," maintaining that these were the very characteristics that were most obvious and brought the Roman authorities to the point of declaring the document subversive and illegal. Clearly sympathetic to this decision by the emperor, Grant states that in his opinion Revelation was nothing more than a document meant to foment revolution.

Fortunately, Grant goes on to say, the Christian church later *did* formulate viewpoints that were much less in conflict with those held by the Roman government. As a result, the relationship between church and state improved and there was better cooperation. Of course there were "setbacks" like the Apocalypse and the "outbursts" of a certain Tatian, a sharp critic of the Roman state. Tatian was of the opinion that "a person ought to be honoured as a person" (and not as a god); to show clearly that he did not recognize the authority of the Roman Caesar, he preferred to speak of "the emperor of the Romans." The fact that this man was declared a heretic by the church in later years makes Grant believe that if church government in the time of John of Patmos had been better organized, "he would also have been convicted" (as a heretic). And all because he disturbed the relationship with the Roman state.

We have spent some time on Grant's argument because it makes the same point we have been pleading for: that the Apocalypse can only really be understood in its political and historical context. Both by the first readers of the Apocalypse and by the authorities of the time, this book was seen as a document with tremendous political implications, a book that stirred those who read it—for the one a well of inspiration and comfort, for the other a source of anger and worry. To read this book differently, as purely foretelling the future or as spiritual escapism into the eschatological world of monsters, dragons, and mysterious numbers, is to misread it—indeed, to distort it.

I find Grant's argument unacceptable when he states that the Christian church subsequently rejected wholeheartedly the way in which John dealt with the subject of church and state relations. First of all, the way in which the Apocalypse is mentioned in the literature of the church fathers, and the obvious esteem in which John of Patmos was held, belies such an argument. Second, the history of the early Christian church teaches precisely that the tensions between the church and the Roman state would remain and, indeed, would lead to open conflict on certain specific issues such as emperor worship and military service. Besides, we can no longer naïvely believe that the advent of Constantine as a "Christian emperor" proved to be a solution to these problems and tensions. Other more dangerous and subtle problems would come in place of the first.

There is an appreciable development in the attitude of the New Testament as regards the issues of suffering and martyrdom. In the oldest portions, the letters of Paul, there is no clear, constructive thinking on the question of martyrdom as such. Of course Paul understands and speaks of suffering, but it is a suffering regarded as being part of the life of the Christian, a suffering the Christian *has* to undergo as a result of the power of sin, of what Paul calls "the flesh." During Paul's life, political oppression and the suffering it brings was clearly not yet so prominent that it merited separate attention.

But in the First Letter of Peter the beginnings of a change occur. Christians are reviled (3:9, 16), there is talk of a "fiery ordeal" (4:12) and of attacks upon Christians. Peter's advice is "to maintain good conduct" (2:12) and to follow the footsteps of Christ, who left an example of suffering (2:21). Christians ought to be loyal to the government (2:13-14) and to know that "one is approved if, mindful of God, [one] endures pain while suffering unjustly" (2:19). Apart from the fact that Peter does make the point that Christians did suffer unjustly (and therefore undeservedly), the element of protest is conspicuously absent.

The persecutions mentioned in the Letter to the Hebrews were apparently perpetrated in a much more systematic fashion than those we read about in the First Letter of Peter. Christians have been imprisoned (10:33-34; 13:3), and the tensions are tangible, even though in the struggle against sin they have "not yet resisted to the point of shedding [their] blood" (12:4). It must comfort them to know that God disciplines those "whom he loves" (12:6). The calling of the Christians under suffering is to remain true under the disciplining hand of God and not give up the faith. "It is discipline that you have to endure" (12:7), for even if it seems painful for the moment, "later it yields the peaceful fruit of righteousness" (12:11).

In the Apocalypse of John, the suffering of Christians as a result of political oppression is the explicit theme. John himself has been banished to Patmos, a Christian by the name of Antipas is killed in Pergamum (2:13), and there is evidence of more victims (6:8). Some have been beheaded (20:4). This kind of persecution makes it clear to John and the church that there is an enemy and that he is real, "drunk with the blood of the saints and the blood of the martyrs of Jesus" (17:6).

With the situation so radically altered, Christians find the advice of Peter that the enemy should not be given offence no longer sufficient. The systematic character of the persecution makes this impossible. The Christian church is now engaged in a life-and-death struggle with the powers of this world, and this situation calls for an unmistakable and unequivocal witness. After all, it is a government which expects the "beast" to be worshipped (13:15; 14:11; 19:20). The dragon makes war on the Lamb and the church (12:17) and on the saints (13:7; 17:14).

Christians are called to follow the Lamb (14:4) and to persist in the faith. Those who remain faithful shall share in the victory of the Lamb over the powers of evil and shall receive the crown of life.

The undisguised hatred the state has for the Christians changes the situation drastically. The martyr is no longer the disciplined son contrasted with the godless state but rather the witness *for* the Messiah *against* the blasphemous state. The church is now partisan of God in the struggle against the powers of evil, for the sake of justice and for the sake of the new creation God has in mind. Both church and Caesar are about to find out that the message of the lordship of the Messiah cannot but challenge, subvert, and call to conversion every evil system. The reactions of the powers that then controlled the lives of the churches, and the reactions of such powers today, testify eloquently to this fact. Like Pharaoh in the time of Moses and the exodus, and like Herod at the birth of Jesus, the power-mad usurpers of this earth know precisely how unerringly the God of the Bible judges them, unmasks their blasphemous pretensions, and puts them in their place. And exactly this judgment is the point at which the dilemma of the oppressor who claims the name "Christian" becomes acute.

"Daniel is an active volcano"

I must say it again: the whole of the Apocalypse is a letter written not for public consumption in marketplaces and city squares but as underground literature, to be read in secret meetings of the Christians, written in a way that would make it as difficult as possible for informers to understand. Under the circumstances, this message of John of Patmos could only have reached his readers through illegal channels. His intention was to comfort, encourage, inspire; by writing a book of protest to call the church to persistent faith and obedience to Messiah, the true *Kyrios*, the only Lord.

Even though this faith was the faith of small, scattered

minorities, it ultimately caused the mighty Roman empire
to fall. In this way the Apocalypse becomes not only a
source of hope for the church of today but also a firm basis
for a Christian liberation theology (Schillebeeckx). In the
fashion of the Apocalypse, our faith becomes a witness—
even unto death—to the right of justice, humanity, and
love to exist in this world. The Apocalypse is determined
to keep the dream of God alive for God's people. It is a
protest against and a call for resistance to evil. It depicts
the dream of a new creation and, for the sake of this new
creation, the unending struggle against eternal destruction, against the primordial monster Leviathan who has
revealed himself from the beginning of the world in the
shape of every power that proves itself an enemy of God
and a destroyer of humanity.

But there lies the secret: it is the faith in Jesus the Messiah who is Lord of combat and of victory, the Lamb who
was slain and is at once the Rider on the white horse. He
himself is in the midst of the struggle, with and for the sake
of his church. This faith seeks neither to avoid suffering as
a consequence of the struggle for the gospel nor to glorify
suffering in some underhanded attempt at self-glorifica-
tion. Those who live in such faith refuse steadfastly to
allow a suffocating fear of death to rule their lives. For in
the midst of all of this the undeniable and unshakable
truth remains: in spite of it all, against it all, above it all,
Jesus Christ is Lord. This has always been the understanding of the Christian church. Hence the remarkable sentence in Eusebius' *Ecclesiastical History* (4.15) concerning
the Martyrdom of St. Polycarp, Bishop of Smyrna:

> The blessed Polycarp died a martyr's death on 23 February,
> on the Great Sabbath, the eighth hour. Herod imprisoned
> him when Phillip of Tralles was the High Priest, and Statius
> Quartus was the pro consul, whilst for ever is King our Lord
> Jesus Christ. His be the glory, honour, majesty, and an ever-
> lasting throne from generation to generation. Amen.

And, indeed, in the world little dictators rule with an
iron hand: Herod, Philip, Statius Quartus, the Caesar.

With boundless arrogance they walk over the people of God. With one stroke of the pen they cause thousands to disappear or die or both; masters of torture do their dirty work for them in dark and dismal cellars while above, in the beautiful halls, they strut to festive music and exchange civilized pleasantries. But the church knows that even as this happens "for ever is King our Lord Jesus Christ." This was true then as it is true now. Nothing is more disturbing for the oppressor than this. Nothing is more comforting for the faithful.

What follows here is biblical exegesis from the underside, reflections on the Apocalypse with the Christian church of today in mind—even more specifically, with the black church in South Africa in mind. As in other times, John's book has much to say to our own times, and especially to those of us who, like the churches of John's time, must live under political oppression. Once again the Christian church is drawn into the struggle between God and the gods. Once again we are forced to make a choice between the living God and the powers of death and destruction. The modern gods of racism, militarism, materialism, and oppressive political and exploitive economic powers confront us with fearsome reality, demanding obedience, loyalty, and slavish submission. As a matter of course they expect from the Christian church loud applause or, at the very least, silent consent. A critical attitude quickly becomes "subversive," the determination of the church to be obedient to God more than to human beings becomes a "threat to the security of the state," and resistance is suicide. Under circumstances such as these, the danger for the church is that our natural tendency to "survive" will totally overwhelm the calling toward kingly protest, priestly comfort, and prophetic suffering.

In South Africa we are blessed—or cursed—with a situation the clarity of which no one can deny. South Africa today has all the characteristics of a police state. There is a persistent effort by the government to bring everything under its control—radio, television, the press, culture, religion, education—everything that can have even a remote influence on the life of the nation. The "security of the state" is already the highest good, and everything must be subservient to it. There is growing militarization of our society and the continued concentration of all political and economic power in the hands of a small power elite. Apartheid with all its horrendous practices continues unabated. The deepest essence of the continuing and growing conflict between the state and the church is the insistence of the government that it is "Christian" and therefore has a mandate from God and that apartheid must be considered a "Christian" policy.

More and more the government is requiring Christians to obey it without question. During the debate in Parliament on the report of the Eloff Commission of Inquiry into the affairs of the South African Council of Churches, the Minister for Law and Order, Mr. Louis Le Grange, warned the churches that it is "dangerous" to continue the teaching that Christians should obey God more than the government. During 1985 the conflict grew. Preachers of the gospel were imprisoned in unprecedented numbers. Church services were banned, and police attacked worshippers with tear gas, dogs, and guns. At my own church such disruptions caused the church council to send a telegram to the Minister for Law and Order and the State President with an urgent plea: "In God's name, please stop this persecution of the church!" There is a continuing attempt by the government to silence pastors. Some are banned, restricted, or charged with treason or subversion. Christians who resist the government on the basis of their faith in Jesus Christ are being persecuted, detained, and tortured. We go to jail by the thousands. It is clear that the government has declared war on our defenceless people as heavily armed police and army troops besiege the black townships and invade our communities, schools, and homes. Soldiers laugh as they beat our pregnant women and terrorize our children. They kill without provocation because the Emergency Regulations give them blanket indemnity.

For people who face situations like these, the Apoca-

lypse is an exciting, inspiring, and marvellous book. It is a
book which, in our sociopolitical situation, is a constant call
to conversion and change. It is prophetic, historical, contemporary. But we shall have to learn to read it differently. We shall have to do away with those sterile escape
mechanisms and dead-end arguments about numbers and
symbols and signs by which the real message of Revelation
is so often paralyzed. We shall have to stop reading the
Apocalypse as if it were meant to be a practical guide to
heaven and hell.

The clue to understanding the Apocalypse as protest
literature—and at the same time the answer to the question as to why so few scholars understand it in this way—
lies, I think, in Revelation 1:9: "I John, your brother, who
share with you in Jesus the tribulation and the kingdom
and the patient endurance [of suffering]." This is the key.
Those who do not know this suffering through oppression,
who do not struggle together with God's people for the
sake of the gospel, and who do not feel in their own bodies
the meaning of oppression and the freedom and joy of
fighting against it shall have grave difficulty understanding
this letter from Patmos. If they think of this book at all,
they will surely have to flee into the wilderness of mysteries, numbers, and symbols. It is the struggling and suffering and hoping together with God's oppressed people that
open new perspectives for the proclamation of the Word
of God as found in the Apocalypse.

So John speaks from his island to the church today. He
confronts us with stark choices: obedience to God and
God's Word or subjection to the Caesar, the Living God or
the one who calls himself god, the Lord or the dragon, the
Messiah king or the beast. The church must choose. Either
we are on our way to the new Jerusalem or we perish with
Babylon. Understanding this is understanding not only
John of Patmos and his church but understanding ourselves, our world, and this Word. It is understanding the
comfort and the protest, the prophetic, hopeful song of
victory that the church already sings, even in the midst of
suffering and fear, destruction, and death.

During the time of Hitler's Germany, pastor Walter Lüthi, one of the witnesses from the Confessing Church, spoke a word of warning to those Christians in Germany who did not seem to understand the signs of their time. They did not understand that in Hitler the beast had once again taken shape, not for the first time but *once again.* And they did not understand that the first duty of the church was to recognize this beast for what it was and to resist. Lüthi's message was clear: Hitler ought to be resisted; he was not to be played with, or ignored, or argued away. "The Apocalypse is upon us," he said. "Daniel is an active volcano."

We are seeing it again, and not only in South Africa. The church must know, as the beasts must know, for the Apocalypse speaks not only of the suffering of the faithful. It speaks also of the destruction of evil and the victory of the Lamb. Indeed, Daniel is an active volcano.

1

The Blessing

Revelation 1

It begins: the revelation given by God to Jesus Christ, made known to John, brother to the suffering little people of God, sharing with them the endurance and sovereignty in Jesus Christ. Times are dark, life is a painful riddle, and history is a sea of injustice, tears, and oppression. There is no peace but the Pax Romana, a "peace" maintained by violence and threat of violence, by the greed of the privileged and the oppression of the weak and the lowly. The church lives in the midst of this turmoil, a time with no understanding and no vision. The people of God knew, however, that this was no true peace. The peace and prosperity of the Roman empire depended on the continued oppression and enslavement of almost 95 percent of the population of the known world. The "peace" was meant for the privileged, the top 5 percent who dwelt in the palaces and courts of Rome.

John writes to Christians in Asia Minor. There, the worship of the emperor, the imperial cult, was especially rife. In the temple in Ephesus, the high priest of this imperial cult bowed down before the image of the divine Caesar and intoned the sacred titles: *Sōtēr, Epiphanēs, Kyrios.* The emperor cult was more than just a religious ceremony. It became an essential component of the state religion and, as such, was intimately linked with the power of the state. To deny the divinity of the emperor was therefore much more than a religious problem. It was first and foremost a political challenge, just as refusal to bow before Nebuchadnezzar's idol had not been so much a religious matter as a political issue, because that refusal became a refusal not to the god but to the king who claimed to be god. Since Christians looked upon their God not merely as a special divinity but as the only true God and redeemer of the world, beside the worship of whom none other might exist, this demand by the emperor was bound to cause the deepest conflict.

It is no wonder, then, that John, pastor to the churches in the Eastern Provinces, found himself in conflict with the emperor and subsequently banned to the island of Patmos for his "preaching of God's Word" and his "testimony to Jesus." On Patmos, fourteen hours by boat from the coast of Asia Minor, John was surely thought to have been disposed of: the regime had succeeded in silencing yet another turbulent priest.

But John and the church—and ultimately the emperor —would discover that John's ministry did not end on Patmos. In reality, it truly began there. The intention was to cut John off from his churches and so undermine his influence. But on that island, John, as never before, found himself experiencing the presence of God and the power of God. This enhanced his ministry, so that he spoke not only to the churches of Asia Minor but to the church of all ages.

Patmos, that infamous island, place of banishment, place of punishment, place of lonely wanderings, became a place of learning, of seeing, of understanding. It became a place of revelation, of discovery, of empowerment. Instead of teetering on the brink of mad isolation, John finds himself drawn to the heart of God and miraculously, wondrously, into the heartbeat of the church, not only of Asia Minor but of the world, not only of that time but of all times to come.

And so, out of the risk of obedience and love for the sake of the gospel and God's people, comes the discovery, the revelation of the heart of God, the unveiling of God's presence. Out of this comes also the speech of joy and hope, of certainty and knowing, of strength and power, of liberation. Patmos, island of shame and imprisonment, is transformed into a place of magnitude and eternal inspiration, a sacrament to the love of the Living One and the faith of the church.

In a single moment in history, the heavens are opened for God's people to see, to understand, and to believe. John is allowed to see what God sees, beyond the darkness of the moment, beyond the tears of the suffering church, beyond even the illusions of glory and power of the mighty Caesar. What John sees is prophecy. It is prophecy not because it simply predicts the future. It is prophecy like all true prophecy: a contradiction of the present *because* there is a vision of the future—God's future. John sees and hears in the voice of the One who speaks to him God's dream for this world and for God's people. John sees visions of love and justice and peace amidst persecution and hardship, hopelessness and despair. John saw that the world was not simply this mad, unsafe place where there was no room for people, for love and humanity. Even in the midst of that naked, frightening reality, he told them, Remember, Jesus Christ is Lord, and he is Lord of life.

Come with me, then, if you will, to a little house in one of the towns of Asia Minor where a small group of people meet in secret. They call themselves *Christianoi*, followers of Jesus Christ. Insignificant still, considered by many to be some kind of Jewish sect, they are sometimes tolerated, but never for long. At this time in their history, they are persecuted; they feel the hot breath of the dragon, they see the teeth of the beast. Clustered around a little lamp in the darkened room, they share bread and wine as the Master has taught them. And then someone rises and reads from a scroll a letter from their pastor, John, no longer with them but banned to the island.

The letter is written in a strange fashion. There are references to beasts and dragons and to Babylon, the great city. Visions, numbers, symbols tumble across the pages. No pagan eavesdropper would understand. No Roman informer would be able to report what was said, because for an outsider it would not have made any sense. But those who have ears to hear, hear now.

Let us change the scene. Come with me to the great hall in Rome, to the palace of Caesar Domitian. It is the Feast of the Seven Hills. As Caesar enters the hall, the court poet rises. His voice rings out, and excitedly the crowd responds, shouting, "Hail, our Lord! Glory, victory to the Lord of the earth! Invincible, crowned with glory, power, and honour. Holy, blessed, incomparable art thou. Worthy alone to enter thy kingdom. Come, O Lord, do not delay. Come!" Caesar enters and the people bow down, for the God of heaven and earth is in their midst. This is Domitian, emperor of Rome and all the world. He has proclaimed himself god; he behaves like a god, rules absolutely, and controls the lives of his subjects with absolute power.

In the year AD 90 the empire receives a new name. It now becomes the Imperium Aeternum, the eternal empire, and the emperor becomes the eternal, everlasting king who will live forever. The Roman court poet Statius says, "You are Lord forever, from eternity to eternity." But of course, court poets are like the prophets of the court of Old Testament times. They do not really prophesy, they merely parrot the wishes of those who pay them. They cannot really see, they have no vision, for Yahweh has closed their eyes and covered their heads (Isa. 29:10). They do not see the agony of God's people, so they do not see God's own tears in the tears and the blood of God's little people. They do not hear any voice except that of their master, and therefore they cannot hear the voice of Yahweh in the cries of anguish of the poor and oppressed. In the end they do not even know. For it is then that they call mere men "god."

We have arrived at the very heart of the conflict. There is Caesar, who claims to be god and expects the obedience and loyalty due a god. He brooks no resistance, tolerates no refusals. And then there is Christ, the Lamb who was slain, the Promised One of God whom the church calls

Messiah and Lord. He is the One to whom the church must be obedient, to whom the loyalty of the church is due, to whom the church owes love. From now on John of Patmos will be locked in battle with this reality. On every page of his letter he will challenge the claims to power, the lies, the half-truths, the propaganda without which no tyrant can survive. On every page he will show the difference between gospel and propaganda, between truth and untruth, between falsehood and prophecy. And he will speak this truth, not as the result of a long intellectual debate but as it arises from within, as he is convinced by his own participation in the struggle for the sake of that truth, by his own pain and suffering with God's people.

"I John, your brother, who share with you in Jesus the tribulation and the kingdom and the patient endurance." Relentlessly, inescapably, these words present themselves as the key to understanding and interpreting what John sees and hears and writes. But it becomes more: the essential qualification for those of us who feel called to preach the gospel. If we do not share the pain and the tribulation of the little people of God, if we do not participate with our prayers and our bodies in the struggles of the people of God, we can hardly be pastors of the church. If we miss this qualification, we can hardly be preachers of the Word. If the pain of the people is merely the pain of our hearts and never the pain of our bodies, we can hardly be shepherd to the people of God. John is prophet and preacher and seer, for he is a brother in suffering.

Breaking the bread and sharing the risks

So, it begins (Rev. 1:4–6):

> Grace to you and peace from him who is and who was and who is to come, and from the seven spirits who are before his throne, and from Jesus Christ the faithful witness, the first-born of the dead, and the ruler of kings on earth.
>
> To him who loves us and has freed us from our sins by his blood and made us a kingdom, priests to his God and Father, to him be glory and dominion for ever and ever. Amen.

To the churches to which John was writing, these words were more than just a formal greeting, such as Paul always gave. They were more than just an exceptionally beautiful liturgical formula. Hear these words as John's people heard them, as oppressed people today hear them. See them as they sit and listen. They were despised, looked down on by the hostile crowds who did not understand or trust their "mad superstition." They were few in number, always on the run, mostly poor and lowly. Every day brought new uncertainties and confirmed the old. Every imperial proclamation might bring new threats. Day after day they prayed that they would be allowed to come together again to share bread and wine. Every time they broke that bread it was in remembrance of him who loved them and whose broken body is the guarantee of forgiveness and mercy, "he who has freed us from our sins." It was a reminder also of the brokenness of his body in the world, a reminder of the broken bodies of brothers and sisters who had been with them yesterday and the day before, but now no longer. They had seen and known the victims of the madness of Nero a scant thirty years ago. They were tortured in dungeons; they fought wild animals in the arena for the entertainment of the beast and his people. Their bodies were used as torches to light up the night so that Caesar could enjoy his sports. "This is my body"— broken on the cross, broken every day in the constant suffering of the people of God, because of their love for God. Now, the nightmare was happening all over again.

Hear these words as they came to these people. They are a reminder of their Lord, who he is, and at the same time a reminder of who Caesar is. It is not true, John says, that Caesar is God. It is not true that he will reign forever. The court poet is lying. That is propaganda. The truth is this: The Eternal One, who is and who was and who is to come, is Jesus Christ our Lord. He, this Jesus, is the faithful witness. His very life and death and resurrection are the realization of the promises of God. In him the promises of the exodus and of the prophets came true. In him the dream of God for justice and peace, for wholeness and

liberation and true humanity, was given life. He is the
servant of Yahweh who shall bring justice even to the ends
of the earth. On him is the Spirit of the Lord, and he
proclaims that the acceptable year of the Lord has come
for the poor and oppressed, the weak and the lowly, the
blind and the lame. This is the light that shone in the
darkness—and no darkness, not even the darkness of oppression under this Caesar, shall overcome it. Jesus is the
faithful witness.

Remember the exodus, John says. And indeed, it is remarkable how the story of Israel's liberation from slavery
in Egypt is a constant shining star in the heaven of John's
revelation. In the moment of Israel's deepest humiliation
and enslavement, Yahweh promised freedom. The people
were reminded that even though for Egypt they were
mere slaves, chattels, cogs in the wheels of Egypt's economy, for this God of heaven and earth they are a kingdom
of priests, chosen for service of the Living One (Ex. 19:6).
This moment of joy and liberation John now invokes. Remember how God's heart was grieved when he saw the
oppression of his people, how afflicted *he* was by the afflictions of his people. Remember his promise: "I have heard
their cry, and I have come down to rescue them from the
hand of Pharaoh, the king of Egypt" (Ex. 3:7–8, para-
phrased).

Listen as Hannah sings another promise, even as God's
promises to her become lifegiving truth (1 Sam. 2:4, 8, 10):

> The bows of the mighty are broken,
>   but the feeble gird on strength. . . .
> The LORD . . . raises up the poor from the dust;
>   he lifts the needy from the ash heap. . . .
> The adversaries of the LORD shall be broken to pieces. . . .
> The LORD will judge the ends of the earth . . .
>   and exalt the power of his anointed.

Listen as Isaiah speaks of visions of peace and justice.
See with him the wild beasts of the earth playing with little
children and lying down with lambs. Listen as Isaiah
dreams with God of the time when people will build their

homes and live in them themselves; when they shall not labour in vain or bear children for calamity (Isaiah 65).

Listen as Mary picks up this promise and repeats it to the generations and to the church to be born into this world out of her love. The One for whom her soul magnifies the Lord is the incarnation of the promise of God. He is the faithful witness.

But he is more. He is the ruler of the kings of the earth. Not Caesar's is the final word the church shall hear, but the Word made flesh. Not Caesar is "Lord" or "Saviour," despite his claims, but Jesus Christ. He is the Alpha and the Omega, the beginning and the end. It is he who through his love has made you a kingdom, priests to serve his God. So to whom do we belong? Whom do we serve? Do we belong to Pharaoh? Even as he challenges the power of the Living One, Pharaoh and his armies and his horses are drowned in the sea. Do we serve Nebuchadnezzar? Even as he builds his image, he learns the truth about himself and the true God in the obedient refusal of three young men. Shall we fear the emperor? Even as the beast raises its head, it must face the Lamb that was slain. For above all kings, however powerful, is Jesus Christ. And he is Lord.

The Word and the words

"Grace to you, and peace" (1:4). It was quite necessary for the church to understand by whose grace it really lived. Domitian had all the arrogant cynicism of the powerful. Whenever he announced a punishment or sentence of death, he began his condemnation with the words, "It has pleased the Lord our God in his grace." Suetonius, Roman historian and biographer of the Caesars, confirms this when he writes, "Domitian prefaced his most savage sentences with the same little speech about mercy; indeed, this preamble soon became a recognized sign that something dreadful was on the way."

By whose grace and mercy do we live? Not by the "grace" of a Caesar, whose "mercy" spells death and de-

struction and inhumanity. We live by the grace of a God
whose forgiveness and love surround us, who frees us from
fear and sin, who affirms the infinite worth of our humanity by becoming a human person.

It is not to be wondered at, this turning around of words
by oppressors of all kinds. We see this every day. The
South African government has laws that prohibit black
families from living together in "white South Africa."
These same laws make criminals out of men and women
who want to be together as husband and wife. This is not
called breaking up families. It is called "influx control" or,
even better, "orderly urbanization." They take the poorest parts of South Africa (13 percent!) and create "homelands" for black people. Then, at the point of a gun, they
forcibly remove black people from places where they
have lived for centuries and send them to these "homelands," where there is hunger and starvation, never-
ending unemployment, and brutal repression by the little
tin gods set up by Pretoria. These places are not called
concentration camps, which is what they are. They are
called "resettlement areas." In these places our children
die of hunger while white South Africa dies of overeating.
Black people are choked to death by hopelessness and
despair, their souls crumbling under the weight of their
powerlessness. But this is not called genocide, it is called
"self-determination."

In order to maintain apartheid, Pretoria declares states
of emergency. Policemen and soldiers have the right to
maim and torture and kill with impunity; a presidential
decree gives them indemnity for now and for the future.
This is not murder, it is called "law and order." In a country which more and more displays the characteristics of a
fascist police state and where even the lighting of a candle
has become a danger to state security, the State President
says in a speech at the opening of Parliament:

> In a world where freedom is becoming increasingly rare, our
> country today is a symbol of the expansion of freedom, of the

upholding of the freedom of religion, sustained by equal
rights before an independent judiciary.

Such is the language of Caesar. It is like listening to
President Reagan say, "We build these missiles not to
make war but to preserve peace." The weapons of total
destruction, the very existence of which is a denial of life
and peace and meaning, become, in the language of Caesar, instruments of peace. Peace is preserved, not through
justice, as the Bible teaches, but through the threat of total
annihilation.

Peace in South Africa is not the active presence of justice, the shalom of God for the whole person and the
whole community, but the absence of protest and the continued suppression of truth. Peace is not bread for the
hungry and security for the homeless, but "stability of the
market" and no tear gas in the white suburbs. "Grace to
you, and peace." No, God's little people need not fear.
They need not crawl into the corners, wondering when
the deadly mercy of this Caesar will end and the rumbles
of this peace will cease. For the people in Asia Minor who
drew comfort from John's words, this was comfort indeed,
just as it is for God's suffering people today. Then, as now,
they did not have power or connections in high places.
They had no certainty except the certain knowledge that
Jesus Christ is Lord.

The church listens and understands anew. It does not
matter what the powers of this world have made of us,
what labels they have put on us—"kaffirs," "niggers," "col-
oureds"—to force us to accept subhuman status and to
hide their own desperate, fearful uncertainty.

The Lord of lords, the King of kings, has made us kings
and priests for his God and Father. The church listens. I
went once to the "independent homeland" of Ciskei, to a
dismal resettlement camp called Keiskammahoek. There
was no food. There was no doctor. I stood by wordlessly as
a young pregnant woman watched workmen from the
Divisional Council dig graves for children estimated to die

during the following week. This mother will not give life; she will give life so that it might die. That is the mercy and the grace of the Caesar who lives in Pretoria.

By what grace does she live? By the grace and mercy of him who is and who was and who is to come. He is the Alpha and the Omega. The idols of this world may think they are omnipotent, but they are no more than idols, "like scarecrows in a cucumber field"—Jeremiah smiles— "and they cannot speak; they have to be carried, for they cannot walk. Be not afraid of them, for they cannot do evil, neither is it in them to do good. . . . The LORD is the true God" (Jer. 10:5, 10).

Nothing angers people so much as when their idols are exposed and destroyed. It is strange how, in the shameful nakedness of the gods, the weakness and utter bankruptcy of their worshippers are revealed and openly put to shame. Their only reaction is anger, fear, and, inevitably, the violence that is second nature to them. "So may the gods do to me, and more also, if I do not make your life as the life of one of them by this time tomorrow" (1 Kings 19:2). This is Jezebel's message to Elijah the day of Elijah's victory over the prophets of Baal. "I warn you," says P W Botha at the end of the first state of emergency in March 1986, "that you have not yet seen the full power the state can unleash." The gods are challenged and exposed, and the battle is on.

"Grace to you and peace from him who is and who was and who is to come, . . . and from Jesus Christ the faithful witness, the first-born of the dead, and the ruler of kings on earth" (1:4–5). To the fearful and persecuted church in Asia Minor, this is a blessing beyond price, a word of protest and comfort from the heart of God. To Caesar, it is a declaration of war. For when the gods are destroyed, the battle is on.

2
The Scroll

Revelation 5

In chapters 2 and 3 of Revelation the spotlight rests on the seven churches of Asia Minor. Each of them is taken seriously in its own right and spoken to in its own particular situation. The seven churches stand for the whole number, for the wholeness of the people of God. To each of these churches, and to the whole church, comes the revealing, incisive word, the admonition to remain true and faithful. To each and to the whole church come also the promises. To those who conquer I will give the tree of life; I will give the hidden manna; I will give power; I will give the morning star. But again and again, the letters end with a reminder: those who have ears, let them hear. But they must hear not the threatening voice of the Caesar, or the persuasive voices of court sycophants, but the voice of the Spirit. Those who have ears—those whose hearts and lives and minds have been captured, have been opened by the Spirit—let them hear and understand and follow.

From the time of Abraham, the people of God have always known this. There is no attempt at explanation or rationalization. It just happens. In the midst of so many other voices, God speaks. Was there a vague uneasiness in Abraham's heart about Haran? Was there some conflict with his environment, or within himself? The Bible does not say. It is only important to know that Abraham felt and believed: *Someone* had something in mind with him. And in the events of his daily life, in the events of history, amidst those other voices, he heard the *voice*. It is no wonder that that whole story of Genesis 12 is dominated by two words: *wayyómer* and *wayyélek:* [God] spoke, [Abraham] went. In this tradition stands the church. The Spirit speaks, and those who have ears to hear, let them hear.

Now, after the letters, comes the scroll. It is a solemn moment. In the heavens a door has been opened. Around the throne upon which the Living One sits are twenty-four elders, representing, exactly as in 1 Chronicles 24, the full tribe of Israel: twenty-four elders called by God to be servants of God for the sake of the people. The elders sing, but there are also other voices. The heavens resound with the voices of the supplicating crowds. In the ears of the church the voices of the poets ring. As Caesar enters it is a sacred moment:

> See, there is God,
> there he is established with supreme power.

The church does not, cannot, concur. It sings another hymn, a hymn of supplication, joy, and defiance (Rev. 4:8, 11):

> Holy, holy, holy, is the Lord God Almighty,
> who was and is and is to come!
> . . . .
> Worthy art thou, our Lord and God,
> to receive glory and honour and power,
> for thou didst create all things,
> and by thy will they existed and were created.

It is this language and this truth Tertullian affirmed when he wrote so much later: "The emperors know full well who has entrusted the empire to their keeping. As mortal men they know who has bestowed life on them; they know that One alone is God under whose authority they stand. . . . The emperor's power comes from the same source as the breath by which he lives." And thus the conclusion is inescapable: "Indeed, I shall not call the emperor 'god.' " Tertullian knew that the twenty-four elders indeed represented the church. When they spoke, they spoke also for him. Their hymn was defiance of Caesar's propaganda but it was more; it was the affirmation of the faith of the church of all times to come.

"And I saw in the right hand of him who was seated on the throne a scroll." It was "written within and on the back, sealed with seven seals" (5:1). Ezekiel had a similar experience. He too was given a scroll written on both sides. It was a book holding the prophecies, the full message God intended Ezekiel not only to preach but to live out amongst the people of Israel. In the same way, the scroll contains the proclamation of the plan of God for this world, the key to the understanding of history. Such heavily sealed scrolls have been found undamaged, and reliefs have survived in which we see the emperor on his throne, the hand with the heavily sealed scroll resting in his lap. A legal Roman will had to be sealed at least seven times, and sometimes the same was true for documents containing top-secret information or some particularly important imperial edict.

John sees a similar scroll in the right hand of the one who sits on the throne. But to his consternation he notes that there is no one, "in heaven or on earth or under the earth," who is worthy to open the scroll. No human being, no angel, no Caesar can open that scroll. By that simple sentence John reminds the church of the limitations of the emperor's power. All the scrolls written by his secretaries, his historians, or his court poets he may open. He may open those scrolls containing his imperial proclamations, believing that the solemn act of opening the scroll in itself is an event that will change the course of history. The scrolls that contain his decisions on the life and death of the little people on whose backs he stands, he may open. But the scroll that contains the secrets of history, the understanding of human life and of God's will for humanity in the world, the scroll containing the promises of God for God's people—the one scroll that matters—he is not worthy to open. He stands, like all other human beings, helpless, not allowed to touch.

Woes and lamentations

Then follows a curious line: "and I wept much that no one was found worthy to open the scroll or to look into it" (5:4). I think his grief can only be understood in terms of the scroll's importance. Like Ezekiel's scroll, this book contains "woes and lamentations," warnings and judgment. And indeed, as the seven seals are finally opened and a new vision is given to John, woes and lamentations rage across the earth, carried forth by four horses, those grim symbols of destruction and catastrophe.

But the opened seals also give a vision of the faithful, slain for the sake of the Word of God. This book must also answer the eternal question, "How long, Lord?" In its pages is the truth about the reality of the church. It contains no propaganda, no euphemisms, no glib party line to keep the party faithful happy. It gives no cheap answers to the painful "Why?" of the church. That scroll must be opened so the church will hear God's voice, in the thundering hoofs of the four horses as well as in the cries of anguish of the souls under the altar. It must be opened so that the church will understand that it is true: God *does* sit enthroned forever, God *has* established the throne for judgment. And God judges the world with righteousness and the people with equity. The Lord *is* a stronghold for the oppressed. The Lord will arise, and mere human beings shall not prevail (Psalm 9).

The scroll must be opened so the church can understand why the people of the world have suffered so much. It must be opened so the church will know that its concern should be not only for the church but for the world. The church does not simply struggle for its own survival but is fighting for the life of the world. If the scroll is not opened, the church will never understand this. If the scroll is not opened, those tormenting riddles will remain unsolved. So John cries. Shall the church never know and understand the meaning of it all? Why must God's children suffer so? Why is it always the innocent, the weak, and the defenceless who suffer first? Why do the powers of this world seem so invincible? Why do they have the right to do with God's children whatever they want? Why does God allow the Neros and Domitians of this world to persecute, to maim and kill? "Exactly why, on 23 February 303, Diocletian signed an edict aimed at outlawing the Christian Church, may perhaps never be known," is a bland, "objective" statement 1700 comfortable years removed from the mud and slime and blood of struggle. Is this all? Has the church no more to say or hear than this? Will history forever be read and understood by the dictates of the powerful and the comfortable?

What of the prophets of God who bring the message of the Living One so that we may hear and understand and respond in obedience and love? Must they be killed and become victims of the very sickness they were trying to heal? Why should Martin Luther King, Jr., the man who taught the United States and the world the meaning of love in action, of sacrifice and hope for our age, die as he did? He stood defenceless in this world, refusing to the very end to take up a weapon against another, so willing was he to be a fool for Christ. Why should he die when his life was just beginning and his message was just starting to be tested in that eternal fire? Why should he die, and with him the dreams of so many? For indeed it is true as it was of Joseph, when his brothers saw him coming: "They said to one another, 'Here comes this dreamer . . . let us kill him . . . and we shall see what will become of his dreams' " (Gen. 37:19–20). Shall the church ever understand?

In the moment that Oscar Romero holds in his hands the chalice and says to his people, "This is the blood of Christ shed for you," an assassin's bullet strikes him down. He was just beginning to understand what it meant, as he himself said, to be "a shepherd of God's people." We saw him giving new meaning to that almost empty phrase, "solidarity with the poor." Why? And what about Steven Biko, that young man who was beginning to teach black people how to walk tall, from whom we learned what "Black is beautiful" means? He became a symbol of our struggle for justice, peace, and human dignity. In spite of that, *because*

of that, he died horribly, painfully, at the hands of policemen who go to church and pray "Our Father." After-
wards, the Minister for Justice, a self-proclaimed Christian, said without blinking an eyelid, "It leaves me cold."
And Christian South Africa, together with its partners
from the Christian civilized Western world, continues
with business as usual. "It leaves me cold." Is there nothing else for the church to say or hear?

Who will answer the mothers of Soweto and Cape
Town, of the resettlement camps and the little rural villages, when they ask why their children had to die? Who
will tell them why they had to bury children dead of hunger in a land where the tables of the rich are groaning
under the weight of too much food? Who will explain to
them why police and army troops hide in a truck from
unarmed, unsuspecting schoolchildren in order to mow
them down with rifle fire? If the scroll is not opened, the
"why" behind the suffering of God's people will not be
heard or answered. It is no wonder John weeps.

The Lamb who was slain

But there *is* someone who is worthy to open the scroll:
"the Lion of the tribe of Judah, the Root of David, [who]
has conquered" (5:5). He is worthy. There are a number
of things here that are important for us to understand.

First, the Lamb, the Lion of Judah, is found *worthy*. It
is not a question of earthly power or might. He does not
open the scroll because he has the ability to enforce or
cajole, to coerce or to deceive. He is found worthy. The
criteria by which Caesar is judged are as nothing here;
they do not count. The Lamb is worthy to open the scroll.
Not Caesar, although poets may address him as *"princeps
principum, summe ducum*—lord of lords, highest of the
high, lord of the earth, god of all things." No, says the
church, worthy is the Lamb, not the Caesar. He is worthy
because his power is so completely different from that of
the Caesar. It is a power not to destroy or to oppress but
a power that is manifested in his love, in his willingness to

give all of himself for the sake of those whom he loves. And in that willingness, in the power of that self-giving love, lies the liberation of his people: "Worthy art thou . . . , for thou wast slain" (5:9).

This is the same insight John the apostle emphasizes in his moving portrayal of the conflict between Jesus and Pontius Pilate in John 18 and 19. It is the same truth the Roman procurator tries anxiously to evade and deny but cannot. The man before him is king, but not at all like the kings of this world. He is a king without armies and weapons, without the instruments of propaganda and deceit, without the pretensions and trappings of power in order to maintain his hold over others. And yet he is a king out of whose sacrificial defencelessness emerges a strength that is the most consistent challenge to the powers of this world. Not clothed with earthly power, yet he undermines and overcomes the powers of this world. In the end, Pilate shall proclaim him king even as he has him nailed to a cross. And the words Pilate causes to be written on the cross are not written to spite the Jews but in spite of himself: *Jesus of Nazareth, King of the Jews.* But even as he does this, Pilate knows the truth. He has tried, but failed, to limit the kingship of Jesus. The Messiah was king, and not merely of the Jews; he was *king.* Pilate knew it then, as the church knows it now. A king like no other, and therefore King. A king whose kingship lies in the truth that he lived and in the life that he gave. "Worthy art thou . . . , for thou wast slain."

The one found worthy to open the scroll and its seven seals is a Lamb. What comes to mind almost immediately is the image of a sweet little lamb—gentle Jesus, meek and mild. Such a notion is appealing, but nonetheless not true, at least not here in the Apocalypse. The word used for "lamb" throughout the Apocalypse is not *amnos,* the word commonly used in the Gospel of John and the First Letter of Peter. In Revelation John of Patmos speaks of Jesus as the *arnion.* This is not the image of the gentle lamb but rather that of the militant little ram, the bellwether. He leads the flock, the first one up on the hill and the first one down in the valley. He has seven eyes, sees all, knows all. Nothing escapes his scrutiny. John echoes the conviction of the faithful throughout the ages: "The LORD is in his holy temple, his eyes behold, his eyelids test, the children of men" (Ps. 11:4).

His eyes are the seven spirits of God; they are at his disposal. On his head are seven horns. Who can gainsay such power? It is not for nothing that the imagery here is so bold. John is preparing us for what is to come. In a short while the *arnion,* the Lamb, will be engaged in battle with the *therion,* the beast. This Lamb is the Lion of Judah, and he stands. The beast does not come onto the scene till chapter 11, but already now the lines are drawn, the stage is set. We should not be surprised when the moment comes.

But there is one more thing. The Lamb stands as though slain. But he stands, he *lives!* He is the one they thought dead and conquered. They thought they had seen the last of him when they shouted, "Let him be crucified!" They really thought it was over when they heard him breathe, "Father, into thy hands I commit my spirit" (Luke 23:46). They thought that Caesar, through the voice of Pontius Pilate, had the last word. If they only knew, John says. See, he lives! He is God's risen One. In Jesus' resurrection God rises up in rebellion against the powers of this world: against evil and sinfulness, against inhumanity and oppression, and against this last final enemy, death, slaying it. Jesus rises up against our rebelliousness against God's will and God's intentions for love and peace and justice. So out of the darkness of the pit he rises, emerging as if slain, but yet alive to lead his people.

He stands as if slain, and yet he is Lord. He is Lord in his suffering, not in spite of it. As the suffering Lord he is the victor over his enemies. He carries the wounds of his people in his body. For their sake he suffered, and in their continuing suffering he is a comforting, gentle, suffering presence. In their afflictions, he is afflicted. In their oppression, he is oppressed. He bears the signs of the suffering they go through still. He is risen, but that does not remove him from his church. With wonder and awe John sees and understands—sees how he bleeds still, with his people. This Lamb who sees all and sees through all, through the dark turmoil of history, through the smoke screens of the powerful, through the veil of tears of the faithful and the just, now steps forward to take the scroll.

In the aftermath of what has become known as Operation Crossroads, where the so-called *witdoeke,* the black vigilantes, supported and armed by the South African police, wreaked havoc and death upon shantytown inhabitants, I went to speak to the people and to survey the complete devastation of what was once Crossroads. What I heard was a litany of grief, a revelation of incredible violence done to defenceless people. I heard from family members how a mother and her four-month-old baby and six-year-old handicapped boy were driven out of their shack by tear gas. As they ran out they were driven back again by gunshots. While they were inside, the shack was set alight and they were burned alive. The police looked on without lifting a finger. The young man who told me the story was barely eighteen. I had no answer to his burning anger, nor had I comfort for the tears of the old woman who stood next to him.

Who will answer the questions that must crowd the mind of the Soweto father as he talks about the death of his four-year-old daughter? "The police say they thought she was a dog, and they shot her. Why did it have to be my little one?" Who else but the One who suffered for her sake could answer this father? Who else could speak to him but the One who became one with us in our pain and need? He who through the darkness of death rose up to rebel against a father's pain and a daughter's untimely death is in reality the One who can really speak to his heart, and to the hearts of thousands upon thousands like him. And maybe he would merely say what he said to Thomas: "Put your finger here, and see my hands; and put out your hand, and place it in my side" (John 20:27). Maybe he will simply say to him, "Be not afraid. See my hands and my feet, it is I."

The joy of the oppressed

It is a wonder that the twenty-four elders and the thousands around the throne are not struck dumb with wonder. But they break out in joy, singing a new song. It is a song of jubilation and of newfound certainty. They know the strife is not over yet.

The battle is only about to begin. Deep valleys of pain and suffering lie ahead. And God's people are still in the midst of the struggle. Yet they sing. It is a joyful noise of victory. It transcends the painful, uncertain present and reaches into the future. Their song overturns the present reality and becomes a prophecy of another reality, God's reality. It penetrates the present darkness and sheds the light of God's vision on the future (5:9–10):

> Worthy art thou . . . ,
> for thou wast slain and by thy blood
>   didst ransom [children] for God
> from every tribe and tongue and people and nation, . . .
> and they shall reign on earth.

And they shall reign on earth! They, these little people, lowly and destitute though they may be, *they* shall reign on earth. Caesar's reign is coming to an end. His oppression has its limits. His time is over. And then they shall reign on earth. "Only a little while," sings Isaiah, "for the ruthless shall come to nought and the scoffer cease, and all who watch to do evil shall be cut off, who by a word make a man out to be an offender, and lay a snare for him who reproves in the gate, and with an empty plea turn aside him who is in the right" (Isa. 29:17, 20–21). It is dangerous, heady stuff, this song. It is a freedom song.

This joyful noise frightens the oppressor. He cannot stand it. Black people in South Africa have made freedom songs part of the struggle; in fact, the struggle is inconceivable without them. Marching down the streets, facing the police and army troops of the South African government, they sing. In jail, they sing—songs of defiance and faith and freedom. It makes the jailers nervous. In prison singing is not allowed, but political prisoners do it anyway, their voices blending as the song is picked up from cell to cell until the prison resounds with music that celebrates the coming victory. Prison wardens, policemen, and heavily armed soldiers cannot understand how people can sing under such circumstances. The more joyful the singing, the more aggressive they become. And so over the last few years we have learned another valuable lesson: The joy of the oppressed is a source of fear for the oppressor. But we sing because we believe, we sing because we hope. We sing because we know that it is only a little while, and the tyrant shall cease to exist.

The song of the twenty-four elders is the same age-old song of Israel, and it vibrates with the same power and certainty (1 Chron. 29:11):

> Thine, O LORD, is the greatness, and the power, and the glory, and the victory, and the majesty; for all that is in the heavens and in the earth is thine; thine is the kingdom, O LORD, and thou art exalted as head above all.

This is the kind of song oppressed people sing with zest and an almost inexpressible joy. Jesus echoes it when he says to the seventy, "I saw Satan fall like lightning from heaven" (Luke 10:18). John hears it and places it in the mouths of "many angels, numbering myriads of myriads and thousands of thousands":

> Worthy is the Lamb who was slain, to receive power and wealth and wisdom and might and honour and glory and blessing!

On a Sunday afternoon young black Christians pick up this ancient song and make of it a new song as they dance around a police vehicle just after a student has been arrested at our church service.

> *Akanamandla, akanamandla, akanamandla uSatani!*
> *Sim'swabisile, Alleluia!*
> *Sim'swabisile, uSatani!*
> *Akanamandla, uSatani!*

In translation it goes something like this:

> It is broken, the power of Satan is broken!
> We have disappointed Satan, his power is broken.
> Alleluia!

As we sing, the song is picked up by others. The police, somewhat confused, somewhat bewildered, somewhat scared, release our friend. Others join us as we march, singing and dancing, back into the church. This is a new song, a freedom song, and the power of it, the sheer joy of it, the amazing truth in it captivate and inspire thousands upon thousands throughout South Africa. For although the seals of the scroll must still be opened, the scroll is not in the hands of Caesar but in the hands of the Lamb. And we will sing this new song until "every creature in heaven and on earth and under the earth and in the sea, and all therein," will say (5:13):

> To him who sits upon the throne and to the Lamb be blessing and honour and glory and might for ever and ever!

Indeed: *Akanamandla, uSatani! Alleluia!*

3

The Seven Seals Opened

Revelation 6–9, 11

The opening of the seven seals is spread over five chapters. In different scenes, working up to a climax, the contents of the scroll are revealed. With the opening of the first four seals, one after the other, at the command of one of the four living creatures, a horse appears. These horses are not sleek, likable animals. Rather, they are wild, heavy creatures, inspiring trembling and fear as they thunder onto the stage of history. They rage across the earth in a frenzy of destructiveness, leaving a trail of blood and suffering behind them.

Horses were instruments of war. For the Jews and the Christians of Palestine, they were symbols of Rome's military might and superior power. Now they become the signs of Rome's destruction—and that of part of the world. The instruments of tyranny are turned against the tyrant. Those thundering hoofs that once heralded the irresistible power of Roman armies are now signalling the inevitable doom of the empire. They become the rumblings of a crumbling kingdom, the groanings of tyranny bleeding to death from a thousand self-inflicted wounds. The erstwhile conquerors shall die in violence they themselves created and can now no longer control. Those who live by the sword shall perish by the sword.

A voice cries "Come!" and a white horse appears. It signifies a war against Rome that the empire evidently loses. The conqueror becomes the conquered, the victor becomes the vanquished.

Upon the opening of the second seal a bright red horse appears. The war is followed by civil war. The enemy is no longer outside, but within. In the bankruptcy of the situation, as the dishonesty and hypocrisy of policies become apparent and the violent "solutions" forced down the throats of others prove to be no solutions at all, they turn upon each other and peace is taken from the earth.

When the third seal is opened, a black horse appears. It brings in hunger and famine, the eternal mates of violence, oppression, and war. Prices are exorbitant: a quart of wheat costs one denarius, a full day's wage. For the poor and the weak, basic foods are out of reach and their situation becomes even more desperate. An unidentified voice says, "Do not harm oil and wine!" There are some who say that this is a (divine) injunction not to dilute the oil and wine with water and sell it as pure. There is another possibility. During the siege of Jerusalem, Titus gave explicit orders not to destroy the oil and wine because he wanted those luxuries for the Romans. Thinking along this line, it makes sense to see this order coming from an unknown voice as John's understanding of what usually happens in such situations. Oil and wine are luxuries to be enjoyed by the rich, who can afford them even in times of want. The black horse states the hard facts of the matter, that the harsh inequalities in distribution of the necessities of life are exacerbated in situations of dire need. God's judgment on this injustice follows in subsequent chapters.

And then the fourth horse is let loose. Its rider is Death. This is not the peaceful death that we all hope for but a death of violence and destruction. This is not death by natural causes, but death as a result of inhumanity, cruelty, hate, and violence. Words of consolation do not help here. No explanation can ever make any sense. All feeling, all hope, is frozen, petrified in that deadly silence that follows the horse of Death: Hades. Death and Hades have, it seems, unchecked power: they kill with sword and with famine and with pestilence and wild beasts no less than a quarter of the people on earth. The destruction is enormous, but not yet total. And the disappearance of the fourth horse is not yet the end.

Some see these horses as descriptions of actual events that took place in the time of John, and, indeed, John may have been referring to events the church experienced. During the last thirty years of his life John actually lived through a series of catastrophes that touched his life and that of the church deeply. There were the earthquakes of AD 60; the humiliating defeat of the Roman army by the Parthians under Vologesus in AD 62; the persecution of the Christians under Nero, which followed the fire of Rome in 64; and the horror of the Jewish War, which lasted a full four years until the year 70 and ended with the destruction of Jerusalem. There was the suicide of Nero, which was followed by chaos as four claimants battled for the imperial throne; Roman legions, loyal to the different opposing contenders, clashed with each other constantly for a full year, while, as usual, the little, defenceless people were pulverized as between great stones. In 79 Vesuvius erupted, obliterating the luxury resorts of the Bay of Naples and creating a pall of darkness so widespread that many feared the imminent dissolution of the physical order. In 92 came the serious grain famine.

It would be wrong, however, to believe that John was writing in symbolic language simply to record these events. If that were the case, he need not have used this kind of language at all. Besides, if this were true, the existing straightforward historical accounts would have been sufficient and John's work should rightly have been discarded as the ravings of a disturbed individual. But the Apocalypse carries a message far more profound. See, John tells his church, how true it is that the wages of sin is death. The continued exploitation of the poor, the oppression of the meek and the lowly, shall not go unchallenged or unpunished. God does indeed judge the nations, and sometimes this judgment takes the form of the inevitable results of people's unwillingness to heed the voice of God. There are clear and predictable consequences for the world if human beings continue to rape the earth and plunder its resources; to exploit, oppress, and dominate the weak and the poor for the sake of greed and the hunger for power; to depend on ever-rising levels of violence and ever more lethal instruments of death and destruction in order to secure positions of power and privilege. Many may see these as the lessons of history. For John and the church it is the voice of God, speaking to the church and the world through these historical lessons and events.

Notice also how much the world suffers because of this. John is responding to the plight of the church, but in reality much more is at stake. John is anxious for the church and the world to understand the indivisibility of our human condition. Injustice *anywhere* is injustice *everywhere*. As long as one person suffers unjustly, the whole world suffers. The existence of injustice, violence, and exploitation contaminates and diminishes the whole human community. The whole of God's creation somehow feels the pain and is in danger. Greed and selfishness threaten not only a few in a certain area but are an onslaught on God's purposes for the whole world. It is right that the incredible, shameful waste of energy in a country like the United States be measured in terms of its effects on the world, and not just in terms of that country's ability to buy those resources. It is right that apartheid be described as a crime, not simply against the black people of South Africa but against humanity. It is a cancer, not merely in the politics of South Africa but in the body politic of the world. The nuclear arms race not only involves the so-called superpowers but is a madness that threatens to destroy the whole of God's creation. It is, as Dorothee Sölle has said, the final onslaught against the very existence of God.

John is not saying that when the church is destroyed the world is also destroyed, in the sense that nothing worthwhile is left. He is saying that the church is in the world, that its history is bound up with the history of the world, and that the life of the church is somehow caught up in the life of the world. The church understands its solidarity with the world and knows how the whole creation "waits with eager longing for the revealing of the [children] of God . . . because the creation itself will be set free from its bondage to decay and obtain the glorious liberty of the children of God" (Rom. 8:19, 21).

The horses are not sent out by God, they are the inevitable consequences of the deliberate choices made by men and women. The first four seals and the horses do not denote natural disasters; the earthquake comes only later. All the disasters described thus far are the result of human action. There are wars in this world, not because wars are the will of God but because of greed and arrogance, the lust for power and domination. There is hunger not merely because there is a lack of food, but because of political and economic policies that foster inequality of the distribution of resources, because of one-sided control of world markets by powerful nations who refuse to enter seriously into the search for a more just, equitable, and sustainable economic order.

There was a time when people of the rich nations of the world regarded poverty as a "natural condition" for those living in the poor nations of the world. Renowned scholar Gunnar Myrdal wrote that the rich accepted the axiom that poor people's "tendency toward idleness and inefficiency, and their reluctance to venture into new enterprises and often even to seek wage employment, were seen as expressions of this lack of ambition, limited economic horizons, survival-mindedness, carefree disposition, and preference for a leisurely life." Christians reassured themselves by reference to the saying of Jesus, "The poor you always have with you." Today we have largely been stripped of this pseudo-innocence. We know that the poor are so poor because the rich are so rich, that the causes of poverty can be traced to deliberate decisions and deliberate economic and political policies designed to benefit the rich and powerful. We now know that poverty and unemployment are not just accidents of history but deliberate, even indispensable, components of capitalism as an economic system.

It is no longer possible for white South Africans or their government to hide behind the grandiloquent ideals of a bankrupt apartheid ideology. Their homeland policy, with its forced removals, relocation camps, deprivation, starvation, and large-scale hunger, is being recognized for what it is: a form of subtle genocide that is not accidental but by design. Shall there be no historic condemnation, no divine judgment for all this? Shall the God of history remain silent? John says no! See, the Lion of Judah, the Lamb who was slain, opens the seals, a voice cries "Come!" and they come, those awesome, grim horses, and on their backs the riders of judgment.

How long, Lord?

The fifth seal is opened, and this time there is no horse and the scene is moved completely, from the earth to the church. John sees an altar and, under the altar, "the souls of those who had been slain for the word of God and for the witness they had borne; they cried out with a loud voice, 'How long before thou wilt judge and avenge our blood on those who dwell upon the earth?' " (6:9–10). The martyrs are dead, but their witness is still alive. Their voices can still be heard; they still inspire the church. They remind the church of what it means to be faithful to Jesus the Messiah, of the price one must pay for testimony to the one true God. They remind the church also of the true character of the powers of this world. The church must not forget who and what it is facing.

It is totally unnecessary to split hairs over whether John meant also to include the martyrs of the Old Testament. The cry "How long, Lord?" has been the cry of the suffering faithful down through the ages. It echoes through the psalms and the prophets, wrenched from the hearts of those who have suffered for their faith and their faithfulness. This cry has mingled with the tears of the oppressed through all times and in all places as they have turned to the Living One as their refuge and strength, their very present help in trouble (Ps. 46:1).

It is a cry of pain and anguish; it is a cry of protest. It is also a cry of hope that God will prove to be the Mighty One, the help of the helpless. In the face of nameless suffering and unnameable gods this cry is a confession: "The Lord reigns!" At the moment of detention; in the long dark hours of incarceration; as the footsteps of your interrogators come down the passage to your cell; above the harsh voices and the scornful laugh; through the blows of fists on tender flesh, the blinding pain of electric shocks; through the hazy, bloody mist of unwanted tears; above the roar of guns and tanks and armoured vehicles; in the nauseating sting of tear gas and the tearing, searing burn of the bullet through your body—the words are shouted, or whispered: "How long, Lord?" It is in the cries of the suffering and the oppressed that the church will hear the voice of God.

It is a cry black South Africans who find their help in Yahweh have been uttering for a long time. They have lived under racist colonial oppression for almost three and a half centuries, and under that particularly vicious form of racism called apartheid for nearly four decades. They have seen their land taken away and themselves stripped of human dignity. Through thirty-eight years of apartheid, group areas, racist humiliation, inferior education, systematic oppression, exploitation, and broken family life to satisfy the white government's "influx control," they have asked, "How long, Lord?" Through these years many have been tortured to death by the police while in detention, policemen laughing behind their hands while ministers gave those well-worn and cynical explanations in parliament and in the press: He died while in the shower, he slipped on a bar of soap; he fell from a ninth-storey window, he committed suicide. "How long, Lord?"

From the earliest days of colonial rule, whole communities have been slaughtered to secure the continuation of white power; and in our time there have been Sharpeville in 1960, Soweto 1976, Cape Town 1980, Langa 1984. During recent years there has hardly been a place where the police and the army have not wantonly murdered our children, piling atrocity upon atrocity for the sake of the preservation of apartheid and white privilege. And as they go from funeral to funeral, burying yet another victim of law and order or yet another killed by government-protected death squads, the cry continues to rise to heaven: "How long, Lord?" How long before this illegitimate power is removed? How long before the blood of our children is avenged? It is a cry, a longing for justice, for comfort, for the final revelation of the truth, clear and undeniable: "The Lord reigns!"

The replies they receive can hardly be called comforting, or so it seems. They are told to "rest a little longer," to endure yet more suffering, to continue to pay the price. No propaganda, no cheap demagoguery or empty bravado of the sort we hear on radio and television day after day. There were no long-winded speeches full of self-pity and threats in yet another attempt by the "Leader" to cover up their fear and mindless desperation. The souls under the altar are told the simple truth: the battle is on, it is not over yet; the price is high, but the end is near. Endure a little longer. All they have is the white robe, that powerful symbol of the certainty that victory is coming. He who gives them the white robe is the Lamb who sits upon the throne. He is one with the God of Israel, whose promises are true and sure. He is one with the God of the exodus, who told the people, "I have heard your cry, I shall deliver you." He is one with the God of the prophets: "I am your God, and you shall be my people. Do not be afraid, for I am with you." He is the Messiah, the promised one of God, and his promises shall never fail: "I am with you always, even to the end of the world. Let not your hearts be troubled."

Rest a little longer, "until the number of [your] fellow servants and brethren are complete." Still more must die; there shall be more blood, more tears, more pain, more suffering. This is true for the people of God who suffer under their persecutor, but this is also true for the persecutor. He shall continue until his deeds are completed. It is strange, almost paradoxical, but nonetheless true. It is like with Pharaoh. God's people are kept in bondage. Pharaoh refuses to let them go, even when God pleads through Moses. "Who is the LORD," we hear him say, "that I should heed his voice?" (Ex. 5:2).

So maybe it is not so strange after all. Is this not precisely the kind of arrogance the powerful always display? Why should they listen to the God of the slaves whose destiny is in their hands? They themselves are gods who preside over life and death. And if one measures power by economic genius and military might, by one's ability to threaten and destroy, to dominate and oppress, why should one listen to a God who makes no higher claim than to be the God of the oppressed and the powerless? God hardened Pharaoh's heart (Ex. 7:13), which means that Pharaoh made his decision and God allowed him to make it. For Pharaoh then, and all the pharaohs of the world since, must learn and God's people must understand. God speaks, but always in the voice of the voiceless, the defenceless, the powerless. If the powerful do not hear God in this way, they will not hear God at all. Then come the plagues. These are clearly economic disasters with profound political implications. But Israel knows they are essentially judgment: "that you may know that there ıs none like me in all the earth" (Ex. 9:14).

This struggle is fought over and over again in the history of God's people. Elijah faces Ahab, Jezebel, and Baal on Mount Carmel, and again the Living One is challenged by self-appointed gods whose throne is based on deceit and falsehood and violence. Elijah knows exactly what the issue is: "Answer me, O LORD, answer me, that this people may know that thou, O LORD, art God" (1 Kings 18:37). "Their idols are like scarecrows in a cucumber field" scoffs Jeremiah, and then moves on to the heart of the matter (Jer. 10:5, 6–7, 10):

> There is none like thee, O LORD . . .
> Who would not fear thee?
>
> . . . .
>
> But the LORD is the true God;
>   he is the living God and the everlasting King.

> At his wrath the earth quakes,
>   and the nations cannot endure his indignation.

But the pharaohs of Egypt, and the pharaohs of Rome, and
the pharaohs of Pretoria as well, never listen. They still
survey their horses and armies, anti-riot equipment and
bombs, and say, "Who is the Lord, that I should listen to
his voice?" And then judgment comes.

It is for this judgment that God's suffering people pray
when they cry, "How long, Lord?" The condemnation of
this prayer in most commentaries is thunderous and immediate. This is not Christian, they say; it is a nullification
of the teaching of Jesus. In *The Revelation of John,* T.
Francis Glasson speaks for most (p. 46):

> If only John the seer had found some way of maintaining the
> principle that love is the strongest power in the world, what
> a great work this would be! But instead, the victory is finally
> envisaged as springing from sheer force; the Lamb changes
> to the Rider on the white horse, sprinkled by the blood of
> his foes, smiting the nations with a sharp sword and gaining
> supremacy by slaughter and divine omnipotence.

People who do not know what oppression and suffering
is react strangely to the language of the Bible. The truth
is that God *is* the God of the poor and the oppressed.
Although they do not count for much in the eyes of the
powerful and the rich, their blood *is* precious in God's
sight (Ps. 72:14). Because they are powerless, God will take
up their cause and redeem them from oppression and
violence. The oppressed do not see any dichotomy between God's love and God's justice. Why is there this divi-
sion between the God of the Old Testament and the God
of Jesus? Why, on this point, does white Western Christianity go back to the heresy of Marcion? God takes up the
cause of the poor and the oppressed precisely because in
this world their voices are not heard—not even by those
who call themselves Christians. God even has to take up
the cause of the poor *against* "Christians." Christians who
enjoy the fruits of injustice without a murmur, who remain
silent as the defenceless are slaughtered, dare not become

indignant when the suffering people of God echo the prayers of the psalms and pray for deliverance and judgment. In the midst of indescribable pain and appalling indifference, this prayer—and the certainty of God's loving response—has become our sustenance. Even as the Louis Le Granges of this world rise up to issue a new threat, we know: "The Lord reigns." *How* God does it is for God to decide. That God *shall* do it is our faith and joy.

Dies irae, dies illa

"Day of wrath, day of terror." These words from the Roman Catholic liturgy *missa pro defunctis* accurately describe the moment of the opening of the sixth seal. Again, most commentators believe that John is thinking of either the actual earthquake of the year 60 or the eruption of Vesuvius in 79 or a combination of both, or that he is merely engaging in the vivid metaphorical speech so typical of apocalyptic writing. We believe John is saying much more than that. Listen to him (6:12–14):

> When he opened the sixth seal, I looked, and behold, there was a great earthquake; and the sun became black as sackcloth, the full moon became like blood, and the stars of the sky fell to the earth as the fig tree sheds its winter fruit when shaken by a gale; the sky vanished like a scroll that is rolled up, and every mountain and island was removed from its place.

This is not an ordinary earthquake, a freak of nature. It is a most powerful symbol. Almost ten times in this piece John quotes the Old Testament: most prominent is Isaiah, upon whose vision John's own vision is based. Isaiah speaks of an earthquake not as a natural disaster but as the symbol of the overthrow of a corrupt and illegitimate political and economic system. It is a litany of judgment on the arrogance of the powerful which we have spoken of before. It is judgment against all their symbols of strength and power, all their political and economic might. Listen to Isaiah 2:12–18:

For the LORD of hosts has a day
    against all that is proud and lofty,
    against all that is lifted up and high;
against all the cedars of Lebanon,
    lofty and lifted up;
    and against all the oaks of Bashan;
against all the high mountains,
    and against all the lofty hills;
against every high tower,
    and against every fortified wall;
against all the ships of Tarshish,
    and against all the beautiful craft.
And the haughtiness of man shall be humbled,
    and the pride of men shall be brought low;
    and the LORD alone will be exalted in that day.
And the idols shall utterly pass away.

Isaiah also knows (34:4) that

the skies [shall] roll up like a scroll.
All their host shall fall,
    as leaves fall from the vine,
    like leaves falling from the fig tree.

The Old Testament often speaks of mountains as symbols of those formidable, unshakable powers that rule the world and dominate the lives of human beings. But on the day of the Lord, upon the unstoppable breakthrough of God's kingdom, those powers that seemed so sure, so invincible, shall crumble and fall. These powers are always hostile to God, which means that they are hostile to God's people. They are the direct opposite of God's power and seek only to oppress. These are the arrogant powers who refuse to listen to the pleading voice of God, and therefore they shall experience God's wrath. The Bible knows that a time may come when God's judgment can no longer be averted (Amos 8:4–7, 9):

Hear this, you who trample upon the needy,
    and bring the poor of the land to an end,
saying, ". . . that we may buy the poor for silver
    and the needy for a pair of sandals. . . ."

The LORD has sworn by the pride of Jacob:
"Surely I will never forget any of their deeds. . . ."
"And on that day," says the Lord GOD,
"I will make the sun go down at noon,
and darken the earth in broad daylight."

Again following Isaiah, John uses the image of people seeking refuge in the mountains and the hills and the holes of the earth. But John's imagery is much more explicit. He is unafraid as he names the enemies of God's persecuted people. Where Isaiah speaks of "men" who shall run to the caves, John is much more direct. And note the "pecking order" (Rev. 6:15):

Then the kings of the earth and the great men and the generals and the rich and the strong, and every one, slave and free, hid in the caves and among the rocks.

On that day there shall be no thought of or comfort in hiding in tanks and fortresses. John makes sure that the myths of strength and invincibility are exploded. Before this God who avenges the meek and the lowly, there is no escape.

The Destroyer destroyed

When the Lamb opens the seventh seal, there is silence in heaven (see 8:1). The pause, as some have argued, is dramatic and effective. But it is more. It is as if all of heaven and earth is holding its breath before the final revelations of the scroll. It is a moment of reverent silence, of realization that the events of history do not just "happen," driven by some grim predetermined force. Somehow, in and through these events, God is there, shaping and challenging, confronting and undermining, subverting and changing human history, working towards the fulfilment of his kingdom.

The opening of the seventh seal brings the images of Egypt, slavery, bondage, and liberation closer still. John will continue to develop the theme of the exodus in great detail as he goes on, a theme well understood by Jewish

Christians, for whom the memory and meaning of Egypt were as close as the laws and decrees emanating from Rome. It is therefore not incongruous at all that the liberation from this new Egypt should be preceded by plagues, begun in chapter 8 and worked out more fully in chapter 15. After all, as we have seen, the differences between the Pharaoh of Egypt and the Pharaoh of Rome are not that great, and, again, it is essential for the people of the church to understand exactly with whom they are dealing. It is true: the Pharaoh of Rome is the Pharaoh of Egypt. But it is also true: the God of the exodus is the God of Jesus Christ. Each plague is God's challenge to the power of the Caesar. Each trumpet blast is a ringing command from the Liberator God: "Let my people go!"

Seven angels, seven blasts on the trumpet, three woes. One word says it all: Abaddon, the destroyer (see 9:11). It seems literally as if all hell has broken loose. The earth and its people are defenceless, doomed to be only victims. What God has created will be torn, ravaged, broken, surrendered to the oblivion that is the relentless power of the one called Abaddon, who is clothed in the terrifying silence of Death and Hades.

And then a curious thing happens. John announces the third woe. "The second woe has passed; behold, the third woe is soon to come" (11:14). But it never comes. Instead, the seventh angel sounds his trumpet and there are loud voices in heaven saying, "The kingdom of the world has become the kingdom of our Lord and of his Christ, and he shall reign for ever and ever." And again the twenty-four elders burst into song (11:17–18):

> We give thanks to thee, Lord God Almighty, who art and
>   who wast,
>   that thou hast taken thy great power and begun to reign.
> The nations raged, but thy wrath came,
>   and the time for the dead to be judged,
> for rewarding thy servants, the prophets and saints,
>   and those who fear thy name, both small and great,
> and for destroying the destroyers of the earth.

So in place of a third woe, we have a song of glory and thanksgiving. Would that third woe have meant the total destruction of the world? But God is not interested in the destruction of the world. The world is God's world, where God's people live. Shall God destroy or allow to be destroyed all God has made in the judgment on the mercilessness of the pharaohs of this world? Is God mindful of a promise made to Noah and his descendants and all the animals of the earth that "never again shall all flesh be cut off by the waters of a flood" (Gen. 9:11)?

Be that as it may, God does not utter the third woe, and the earth is not destroyed. God destroys the destroyers of the earth, the murderers of God's children. The earth is safe and shall be renewed, and the church bursts out in song, for the kingdom of the world, that which has been claimed unjustly by Satan, that kingdom usurped by the forces of death and destruction, belongs now to God and to Christ, who shall reign forever.

Even so, the central theme of these chapters is not victory but the ongoing struggle; it is not vengeance but judgment, not final freedom but freedom in pain and suffering. It speaks not of the glorious end but of endurance and quiet courage. The church is torn between sadness and joy, between the heaviness of the moment and the hope for tomorrow. It is amazed at the destruction sin can cause, and it is amazed at the steadfast mercy of the living God. It is bewildered at the persistence with which human beings turn away from God and choose death over life, and it understands: the Pharaoh is not yet dead. The plagues will come, again and again, before the end.

But John has not yet finished. In heaven God's temple is opened, "and the ark of the covenant was seen within" (11:19). The ark of the covenant is the symbol of God's presence in the midst of his people, the seal of God's promises that will never fail. "I am the LORD your God, who brought you out of the land of Egypt, out of the house of bondage" (Ex. 20:2). The covenant promises: "I shall be your God. You will be my people." The covenant affirms:

"And it shall be that whoever calls upon the name of the Lord shall be saved." The covenant declares: "Therefore the LORD waits to be gracious to you; therefore he exalts himself to show mercy to you. For the LORD is a God of justice; blessed are all those who wait for him" (Isa. 30:18).

For the moment, this long-drawn-out, pain-filled moment, this is enough.

4

The Woman and the Dragon

Revelation 12

Chapters 12 and 13 mark the beginning of an incredible drama, of a struggle of cosmic proportions. There are three dramatis personae: the woman, the dragon, and the child. All three are well-known images in apocalyptic writing and always portray specific realities, for those who write as well as for those who read. As he does so often, John reaches back again into the history of Israel to interpret the situation of the church in the world of his day. The powerful paradigm of the exodus is taken a step farther.

> And a great portent appeared in heaven, a woman clothed with the sun, with the moon under her feet, and on her head a crown of twelve stars; she was with child.

The woman is the image of the people of God, the Messianic community out of which the Messiah is to be born, and she faces, alone and defenceless, "a great red dragon, with seven heads and ten horns, and seven diadems upon his heads" (12:3). The very intent of the description seems to be that we should not try to picture this monster, so horrific is he. On his heads are symbols of royalty and dominion. In his monstrous hellish power and malignity, the monster arrogates to himself power we cannot even imagine. As demonstration of this power and his willingness to use it, and surely to crumble any resistance beforehand, "his tail swept down a third of the stars of heaven, and cast them to the earth" (12:4).

I can think of three reasons why the dragon sets out to kill the child. The first reason lies in the fact that the woman is pregnant, for that alone is an indication that the dragon has lost before the battle has truly begun. Almost from the very beginning the biblical writers knew the contrast and tension between barrenness and the gift of having children. Barrenness is the way of human history without God. It is hopelessness, powerlessness, joylessness. It is to be without a future and without human power to invent a future. Wherever this theme appears, it is laden with depth and meaning far beyond the circumstances of the story—Sarah, Rebecca, Rachel, Hannah. And always the future of God's people—nay, more, the truthfulness of God's promises—is at stake.

"But barrenness is not only the condition of hopeless humanity. The marvel of biblical faith is that barrenness is the arena of God's life-giving action," writes Walter Brueggemann. And as Yahweh steps into this hopeless, barren void and speaks a word of life which gives life to his promises and creates a future for his people, a major victory is won over the forces of death and despair. Already it is clear: not hopelessness but hope and joy shall triumph, not death but life shall reign. God ends the barrenness of Israel and Sarah gives birth to Isaac, a living, tangible sign of promise. And again, into the barrenness of slavery and bondage in Egypt comes God's life-giving and liberating word, and the exodus is living promise and life-giving reality.

A second reason for the dragon to kill the child is that the woman's pregnancy is a sign that God has already taken up the fight for her. She is indeed defenceless, but the living and life-giving God is her helper, and *therein* lies her strength. Listen again as Hannah, the defenceless pregnant one, sings of her Lord (1 Sam 2:1–2, 9–10):

> My heart exults in the LORD;
>   my strength is exalted in the LORD. . . .
> There is none holy like the LORD

> there is none besides thee;
> there is no rock like our God.
>
> .   .   .   .
>
> He will guard the feet of his faithful ones;
>   but the wicked shall be cut off in darkness;
>   for not by might shall a man prevail. . . .
> The adversaries of the LORD shall be broken to pieces.

The third reason lies in the fact that her child will give life to the world even as the woman gives life to the child. To bring life to a lifeless world means to break the hold of the dragon over this world. The child will teach the world the meaning of real, meaningful, truthful life. Because that is so, all life in the world that depends on power and might and destruction and fear will be exposed, unmasked as meaningless, as lifeless as death. And because this is so, the dragon knows of only one solution: the child must die.

The woman is as defenceless against this dragon as Israel was against Egypt. She is defenceless and weak, but she is the bearer of life and hope. Besides, it is in loving and giving life that one is most vulnerable. Israel's new birth through the exodus meant a new life, away from slavery and bondage, in the freedom of the service of the Living One. It meant leaving Egypt, land of enslavement and death, and walking in the footsteps of God to the land of promise and life. It meant leaving the "security" of Egypt, which was based on servitude and violence, and taking the risk of freedom and obedience, depending on nothing else but the promises of the Lord. Listening to that *voice*, walking away from Egypt, was the public denouncement of the power and the gods of Egypt which were—how could it be otherwise?—Pharaoh. In taking that risk, Israel was most vulnerable, but it is a vulnerability which comes of God and which in the end is strength and power and glory.

The wilderness is once again the hiding place; it offers protection. It is the place to which Israel flees after the exodus. It is also a place in which to learn to depend entirely upon God and God's promise. It is the place where God gives Israel bread; more than that, it is the place where Israel receives the Ten Words—ten words of life

without which no true human life is possible. For even
then Israel knew that one shall not live by bread alone. So
although the wilderness can often be a place of fear, deso-
lation, and temptation, here it is a reminder of the place
where God offered Israel shelter and protection against
"the great dragon that lies in the midst of his streams," as
Ezekiel speaks of Pharaoh (Ezek. 29:3).

John is meticulous in drawing the analogy. The time of
the stay of the woman in the desert is 1260 days. This
equals forty-two months and corresponds with the forty-
two stages of Israel's trek through the wilderness, about
which we read in Numbers 33. The fullness of God's love
and protection shall be the woman's until, so to speak, her
journey is completed.

All this John applies to his own situation, and his readers
relive once again the power of the story of Israel's liberation. There is God's people, the Messianic community out
of whom the Messiah, the promised One of God, is to be
born. This birth the dragon cannot prevent, and the child,
who will rule with a rod of iron, gives life to the world,
becomes the life and light of the world, and the darkness
cannot overcome it. The dragon is the great enemy of God
and God's people. John is not directly speaking of the
human personification of evil; that comes later. Here he is
concerned with the power *behind* Pharaoh, or Herod, or
Caesar: the devil, the serpent, the ancient enemy of God
—the deceiver and liar, the accuser of God's children, the
destroyer who cannot stand life and love and freedom.

As defenceless and powerless as the woman is against
the dragon, so is the church in the midst of the powers of
the world. The church does not understand, nor does it
seek to understand, the ways of worldly power. The
church does not seek to master what is called the power
game, nor employ what the world calls power. There is no
question of becoming the world's equal in this regard, of
finding an equal stand where we can be as strong, as
threatening, as powerful as the world. For the power the
world seeks is the power to dominate, to oppress; it is a
power "over others" (see Matt. 20:25). The church seeks

power that is not *over* others but *with* others, power not to destroy but to build, not to dominate but to share, not to oppress but to liberate. True power is not the ability to claim but to serve. It is not the ability to destroy life in order to survive or feel secure, it is the ability to give one's own life so that others may live.

When we are willing to give up our life, the power of the world is truly unmasked as powerlessness, as mere brute force, and therefore inauthentic. The church should really know this. But we don't. We are far too busy imitating the power structures of the world in the life of the church. We really believe that the highest power in the church lies with bishops, moderators, and secretary-generals instead of in the daily risks of faith and obedience taken by the little people of God in the streets. We are far more interested in speaking with the government than in speaking with the people. We send "high-powered" delegations to meet the "high-powered" delegation from the government. We do not know what we are doing. If we cannot understand these elementary things, how can we understand the joy and the anguish in that blessed paradox of true discipleship: giving one's life in order to save it in the life of others and the triumph of good?

But this is precisely what young blacks are teaching the church in South Africa today. Their statement directed at the South African government, "You can only kill us," is not simply the innocent, unthinking bravado of youth. *That* particular innocence was indeed displayed in 1976; we did not expect the South African government to react with such incredible violence to the nonviolent resistance of the young generation. Neither did we expect the horrific, cold-blooded murder of our children. That innocence was shot to pieces on the streets of Soweto. We now *know* what the South African government is capable of doing in order to maintain white oppression in our country. What we are learning is the truth that in order for a new South Africa to be born, we have to be willing to give up our lives. We are learning the meaning of the reply to the souls underneath the altar. And in the process we have exposed the true nature of the South African state. Their only power is the power to destroy. They can never last. If the church as a whole in South Africa does not learn that now, soon it will have nothing to teach.

War broke out in heaven

"Now war broke out in heaven" (Lenski). John writes this with a nonchalance that is staggering. Either we follow the vast majority of commentators who spiritualize this war into absurdity, or we look for a way closer to John's meaning. John is expounding a truth that is basic to the biblical message and yet unpalatable for many. John is saying what Israel discovered in the exodus: this God in whom the church believes, out of whose love the church lives, upon whose mercy the church stands, does not and cannot leave the church alone. This God refuses to remain aloof while God's people are locked in battle with the forces of evil. God becomes passionately involved when God's people suffer and struggle for the sake of the truth. And when they cry out the heavens are disturbed.

It is not true that the peace and bliss of heaven cannot be turned into battle, as some claim. John is saying exactly the opposite! The heavens *are* disturbed, even as Jesus was torn when he saw the suffering of God's people in the world. Isaiah knows better than modern commentators the relationship between God and God's people. He knows that "in all their affliction he was afflicted" (Isa. 63:9), and he knows what it means to pray, "O that thou wouldst rend the heavens and come down, that the mountains might quake at thy presence" (Isa. 64:1). This happens at the exodus, and how Egypt, that mighty mountain, quaked in the presence of this Liberator God! John believes it will happen again.

Over and over the Bible rejoices in the truth that God cannot and will not simply stand on the sidelines and remain neutral. Neutrality is leaving things up to the dragon —no, taking the side of the dragon. And so in the struggle for shalom, for justice, for humanity and the true life of the church and of the world, God takes sides, becomes involved, makes war on behalf of God's people. Right down through the centuries the Pharaohs, the Nebuchadnezzars, the Ahabs, and the Herods have discovered to their peril that they were not simply facing weak, powerless slaves. They have engaged in battle with the living God of heaven and earth who is afflicted in the affliction of God's people and wounded in their wounds. In God's presence the persecutors will disappear, "as when fire kindles brushwood" (Isa. 64:2).

The prophets proclaim this and the psalmists sing about it. In the struggle between Elijah and Ahab, Elijah not only represents God, he also represents Naboth, a symbol of the weak and defenceless, powerless against the power and greed of the king. And in taking the side of Elijah so that all Israel can know that Elijah speaks for God, God takes also the side of Naboth, wronged, robbed, murdered. In the struggle of the prophets against the rich and powerful in Israel for the sake of the poor and oppressed, God vindicates the prophets by taking up the cause of the poor for the whole world to see. God *is* a stronghold for the oppressed (Ps. 9:9); God *does* defend the cause of the poorest, give liberation to the needy, and crush their oppressor (Ps. 72:4). John believes it will happen again.

The one who takes charge in this war on the side of the heavenly hosts is Michael, whose name immediately takes us back (again!) to the story of the exodus. *Michael* means "Who is like God?" Again the church hears the proud, arrogant question of the all-powerful Pharaoh: "Who is this God, that I should listen to his voice?" Again the church is reminded of God's intention: "That you [Pharaoh] may know that there is none like me in all the earth" (Ex. 9:14). In the struggle against the powers of evil, the church is small and defenceless. The little people of God are no match for the strong, proud, arrogant men with the medals and loud voices and weaponry. Their menacing presence seems to fill not only the earth but the heavens too, and the insane clamour of their armaments is all around us. Behind them the dragon rises up and shakes

the stars with his preventive show of force in order to
intimidate the faithful. The struggle is uneven; it seems
that the battle will be lost even before it has begun. The
appearance of Michael changes all this. His very presence
is an announcement of the power of God, a question
whose answer is already given. The answer is given in the
exodus, in the actions of God in history for the sake of
God's people, in the resurrection of Jesus, in the coming
liberation of the church. In spite of Pharaoh or Herod or
Caesar, Michael's presence already represents victory.
Who is like God? The church can only answer with the
prophets: "There is none like thee, Lord."

Again: the blessed paradox

The appearance of Michael and his angels does not mean
the end of the battle. To the contrary, the dragon is extraor-
dinarily combative. He knows that the birth of this child
constitutes a threat to his power. He will not give up his rule
without a fight. But he is defeated, he and his angels, "there
was no longer any place for them in heaven." The first
battle is won, and, at least in heaven, there is no more room
for him. What he has unrightfully claimed in the first place
is now reclaimed by God. John calls him by all his names
and therefore names all his works: the ancient serpent,
Devil, Satan, deceiver of the whole world—he is over-
thrown, conquered, thrown down to earth.

In the understanding of the early church, this is what
Jesus Christ had done in his battle against the powers of
evil. In his life, death, and resurrection he had conquered
or, in the words of the writer of the First Letter of John,
"destroyed the works of the devil" (3:8). Jesus came, not
simply to pour oil on our wounds or cover up the sinfulness
of the world. He came to destroy the works of Satan. He
did this not by matching the power of Satan with equal
power; not with propaganda or violence; nor with the
simple, pietistic sentimentality of the sweet, gentle Jesus
invented by Western Christianity. He did it by his incarnation, his identification with the poor, the meek, and the

lowly; by his engagement in the struggle for God's kingdom of shalom and justice and love, even at the price of his life. In the life and death and resurrection of the Messiah, more than in anything else, God's radical involvement in human history becomes clear. All this is reflected in Michael's war against the dragon. The Devil understands: if he will not give up his rule without a fight, certainly God will not give up the people, the world, or God's own purposes for the people and the world without a battle.

And now again there is a song of praise. Many make the mistake of interpreting this song, as they do the other songs in this book, in a purely triumphalistic fashion. Others ask if it is not premature to sing when the battle is not yet over. Neither view is correct. Oppressed people in South Africa understand the need for singing. Sometimes a song is a song of triumph, celebrating a success, expressing hope that the ultimate victory will come. It is a song of anticipation. Other songs express mourning, ask painful questions that cannot easily be answered. Still other songs simply express the reality of our situation. This reality is not merely discussed or analyzed intellectually, it is sung and, by being sung, is brought into the sharpest focus not only in our minds but also in our hearts. Such a song is the song of Revelation 12.

This song has nothing to do with the shallow, triumphalistic "Jesus-is-the-answer" theology with which oppressed people are so often taught to comfort themselves. Neither is it premature, for the battle is won, even though the struggle is not yet over. And besides, it drives the dragon crazy when you sing about his downfall even though you are bleeding.

The song falls into three parts. "Now the salvation and the power and the kingdom of our God and the authority of his Christ have come" (12:10). The battle has been won, even though it may take time for the end to come. In principle, the dragon has lost. We are engaged, then, not simply in a struggle but in a struggle which has to end in final victory. Note how John pinpoints all the attributes

Caesar (as representative of the dragon) claims for himself: salvation (liberation), power, kingdom (rule, lordship), authority. These, he tells the church, do not belong to Caesar, not even to him for whom Caesar acts; they belong to our God and to Christ.

The second theme is sung with fear and trembling; it is sober and quiet, almost chilling. "And they [our brethren] have conquered him by the blood of the Lamb and by the word of their testimony, for they loved not their lives even unto death" (12:11). God's victory is also the victory of the saints. Two things claim our attention here.

First, there is a war on; there is a struggle. There is a fight for justice, peace, freedom, and reconciliation. These are not things that come to us on the wheels of inevitability. They must be fought for.

Reconciliation presupposes alienation, from the Living One and from one another. To be reconciled means to face the truth about ourselves and about the things we do to each other. It cannot mean covering up the truth because it is too painful. It means confrontation with the evil in the world, the evil within us. Can white and black South Africans be reconciled without facing their history of three and a half centuries of oppression? Can we be reconciled without facing the children who die of hunger while white South Africans die of overeating? Dare we face a future together without coming to terms with the past and the present, with the humiliation and the pain, the suffering, the prisons, the torture, the murder, the massacres? Seeking reconciliation means facing the guilt and knowing the need for forgiveness. In order for Christ to reconcile the world with God, he had to die on the cross. What makes us think we will get away with less? The reconciliation we need is costly. It is won only through the pain of struggle.

Freedom, justice, peace are the antithesis of the reality we live with. They will become reality in South African life only if we fight for them. The forces of evil would keep our country the way it is. But we have another vision: the end to apartheid and racism, bringing openness and freedom, an end to hatred and bloodshed, bringing peace for our children so that it will no longer matter that one is black and the other white. But these things must be fought for. In his book *Ah, But Your Land Is Beautiful* (pp. 66–67) Alan Paton introduces a cautious middle-class black man who belatedly joins the struggle. To his bemused white friend he explains, "When I go up there, which is my intention, the Big Judge [in heaven] will say to me, Where are your wounds? and if I say I haven't any, he will say, Was there nothing to fight for?"

The second thing we must take note of is how the saints triumphed: "By the blood of the Lamb and by the word of their testimony, for they loved not their lives even unto death" (12:11). Here John first of all affirms the testimony of the church; Jesus Christ, in his death and resurrection, has won the victory over Satan. In him it has already happened. But it has to be affirmed by those who believe through their own testimony, their lives, their deeds, which proclaim the liberation Christ has given them. In doing this, they understand that although life is precious, they should not cling to it at all costs, at all times. This call to the most radical form of discipleship is the most difficult of all. And yet there is no other way.

We think of Dietrich Bonhoeffer, of Martin Luther King, of Oscar Romero and Steve Biko, of Kaj Munk and Olof Palme. We think of Matthew Goniwe, Sparrow Mkhonto, Ford Calata, and David Mhlawuli and many otners in our country who have given their lives in the struggle for justice and liberation. One stands at yet another grave and thinks, This is what I must be prepared for —and one trembles. We hear again the threatening voices and see what is happening, and we rise up in anger at those who speak so glibly of martyrdom. We get even angrier at those who, while hiding behind the guns of the oppressor, accuse us of seeking to become martyrs. There is no way to explain this to those who will never understand what it means to know that life may be all one has, but it is not all there is. We love life because it is a gift of God, we protect it from the destroyers of the earth because it is sacred, and yet we are willing to give it up for the sake of others because giving it thus is a gift of God too. The third theme of the song is as much sober reflection as warning. "Rejoice then, O heaven and you that dwell therein! But woe to you, O earth and sea, for the devil has come down to you in great wrath, because he knows that his time is short!" (12:12). The theme is carried by the blessed paradox we have talked about. The devil is conquered, we have seen it, but the struggle is not yet over. The battle is won in heaven, but it is yet to begin in all earnest on earth. Even as the church rejoices in the first victory, it prepares for difficult days ahead. The devil has come down "in great wrath" because he has lost, but also because he knows his time is short. And precisely because his time is short he will do as much damage as he can.

How well do we know that! The South African government's time is up. That we know. We are seeing the beginning of the end. But that does not stop them. Still they invent new weapons, which they display with great pride at the Arms Fair in Brazil. Still they announce newer, more refined anti-riot equipment: instant barbed-wire fences falling out of the back of a truck like deadly vomit out of the mouth of a dragon. Still they legislate new powers for the Minister for Law and Order to declare any area an "unrest area," which means an emergency area without officially declaring a state of emergency. But oppressed people know what that means: the respectability of "law" for wanton destruction, unending streams of arrests, besieged townships, invaded communities and homes, fear-ridden streets, thousands of policemen and soldiers, grim and wild-eyed as they feverishly grip their guns—in a word, legalized murder. Indeed, how well John knows it. Woe! Oy! Prepare yourself, for he knows his time is short. But then again, rejoice! For we know it too.

The struggle continues

As the dragon sees that he has lost the battle in heaven and is thrown down on the earth, he turns his rage on the woman once more. But she is in the care of God and escapes on the wings of an eagle. John never loses the thread of his narrative. Just as Pharaoh had given orders to drive the children of Israel into the sea, so the dragon spews forth a great river of water to drown the woman. It is almost as if John's congregation spontaneously pick up the words as the exodus story unfolds: "You have seen what I did to the Egyptians, and how I bore you on eagles' wings and brought you to myself" (Ex. 19:4).

As this last desperate attempt to kill the woman fails, a curious thing happens. John puts it down without any explanation. "But the earth came to the help of the woman" (12:16). I do not know how to understand this sentence unless it means that apart from divine intervention, in the struggle against the forces of evil, ordinary, earthly things come to the aid of the children of God.

For example, in South Africa, the curse and, for Christians, the deepest pain of apartheid has always been the claim that the policy is "Christian." For years, white Dutch Reformed churches worked on the theology of apartheid, distorting scripture, concocting arguments from the Bible in defence and justification of that evil system. All of a sudden, out of the blue as it were, came the action of the General Council of the World Alliance of Reformed Churches, held in Ottawa, Canada, in 1982. It is not as influential a group as the World Council of Churches; its actions are never taken as seriously. But this body declared apartheid a sin, and its theological justification and persistent disobedience to the Word of God a heresy. The impact went beyond anyone's expectations. Suddenly the South African system was stripped of its moral claims, the churches who supported it standing exposed and shamed. All that was left were the naked greed, the lust for power, and the desperate fear.

Consider a second example. For years, "banning" has been a favourite, extremely effective, albeit despised tactic of the South African government. A banned person may not leave a certain geographical area, may not be quoted, may not publish, may not enter the premises of

certain stipulated institutions, may not speak with more
than one person at a time, may not attend any political,
social, or church gathering. The government went to a lot
of trouble to make sure that this form of silencing their
opponents was covered by legislation, and merely reading
those laws is a drain on one's spirit. But these people are
human, and in 1985, in their haste to have as many people
banned as possible, they made some mistakes that were
picked up by a vigilant lawyer, who then had the courage
to challenge one banning order in court. To everybody's
surprise, and to our delight and the government's chagrin,
the appeal was upheld and the banning order was declared invalid. A lawyer had seen the possibility, and a
judge had the moral courage to challenge the beast. As a
result, the government was forced to lift the remaining
banning orders in order to avoid more open humiliation
in court. It still happens: the earth comes to the help of the
woman, and the children of God rejoice.

But there is still verse 17: "Then the dragon was angry
with the woman, and went off to make war on the rest of
her offspring. . . . And he stood on the sand of the sea." The
church has been warned. The battle is not over yet; a new
phase is about to begin. The dragon is still very much alive.
Angered beyond words, he stands on the sand of the sea.
And waits.

5

The Beast from the Sea and the Beast from the Earth

Revelation 13

The drama continues. The woman, so we saw, is safe; the dragon is at large and is about to employ a totally new strategy. Now the two beasts arise, one from the sea and the other from the earth, and they have everything to do with the dragon. The final onslaught is about to begin.

We should pause a moment to clarify our stand once more. Chapter 13, more than any other in Revelation, has been subject to the wildest and most fanatical speculation. I cannot agree with the widely held futuristic view that projects all that is happening here into the distant future. And for Hal Lindsay and Ronald Reagan, that time is now. "I don't know about you," President Reagan has said, referring to what he believes to be the prophecies spelling out the end-times, "but I certainly believe those times are here." However, biblical prophecy and prophetic vision are not fortune-telling but insight into history. John understands that what is happening in his time has happened before and will happen again. What he sees is not the culmination of a process but a *condition* of human history, a condition that will reveal itself again and again in other times and other situations. The two beasts were active before John's churches met them, they are alive now, and they will continue to reveal themselves in all their frightening power and mercilessness until the final victory comes in Christ.

I disagree also with those who hold that these visions

reflect only a small part of history, that of John's time. They believe that John is describing only those emperors he knew, in particular Caligula, with his reign of three years, ten months, and seven days, or Nero and the legend of his return from the dead. But the visions of John are more than just a "Christian" record of contemporary history. His book is prophecy, and therefore it reflects depth and understanding that go beyond the mere recording of events. His visions are visions of prophetic insight; he knows that Nero and Caligula and Domitian are only *manifestations* of this condition of human history. Over and above this condition, and over and above the roar of the beasts, there is God, whose love for the people never fails, and whose judgment remains true and faithful. Vivid as John's awareness is of the power of the beasts, his faith in the faithfulness of this God is unwavering.

A crown and a blasphemous title

"And I saw a beast rising out of the sea." In the Bible the sea is not a friendly provider of life and sustenance, nor is it seen as a thing of beauty and romance. The sea is the nether reservoir of evil, the abode of Leviathan. Its eternal restlessness is the restlessness of a monster on the prowl, forever moving, forever threatening. Out of these cosmic depths Daniel saw four beasts arise, among them a grim, nameless horror with ten horns, "terrible and dreadful and exceedingly strong; and it had great iron teeth; it devoured and broke in pieces, and stamped the residue with its feet" (Dan. 7:7). Out of this sea John of Patmos sees a beast arise with the characteristics of all four of Daniel's beasts.

The description reminds us of a royal personage. John has in mind a state or the personification of state authority. There is no doubt that for John and the church this beast represented the imperial authority. It has seven heads, symbolizing the succession of seven Roman emperors. The ten horns represent the ten subject kings who do the bidding of the beast. Among them it is the first and most important and claims the title "king of kings." Their presence emphasizes its power.

Each of the heads bears a "blasphemous name." On the imperial coins that circulated throughout the realm, the heads of the emperors appeared, with their blasphemous names. Almost all were declared divine at death, and in the eastern provinces, where the official language was Greek, the coins bore the title Theos (God), which could have left no doubt in the minds of either Jews or Christians as to the emperors' intentions. Domitian, as we saw, went further and wished to be called "the Most High One," "Lord and God," "God of all things." He was all-powerful and completely without mercy. The people knew that and blindly they followed him; without question they obeyed him. Any form of resistance was suicide.

The emperor has been idolized. But make no mistake, John says, all humanity has fled. This ruler knows no human feeling or understanding. It is no longer possible to have a human relationship, for there is no human feeling to appeal to. He is, quite simply, a beast.

This revelation is as startling to us as it seems to have been obvious for John. Why is the state authority here described as a beast? Does not the Bible speak differently about the authority of the state, as we so clearly see in Romans 13:1–7? It is right that these questions are asked, if only because we believe there is much misunderstanding about Romans 13, as there is about Revelation 13 and the relationship between these two passages of scripture. Much of the misunderstanding arose because Christians have persistently read Romans 13 as an unquestionable legitimation of state power, which has resulted in the blind, unquestioning obedience of Christians to the state. Misunderstanding also arose because of fanatical speculation about the meaning of Revelation 13, to which we have alluded at the beginning of this chapter. But there is also misunderstanding because so many do not even see, much less understand, the relationship between these two passages. They are in tension, not in conflict with each other. Revelation 13 is in the Bible *because* Romans 13 is in the Bible.

As I pointed out in *When Prayer Makes News,* published as *A Call for an End to Unjust Rule* by St. Andrew Press, in the chapter "What Belongs to Caesar?" (from which much of the following argument is taken), the difficulty with Romans 13 arises almost at once, with verse 1: "Let every person be subject to the governing authorities." This sentence, often cited as requiring unquestioning obedience to the government, is actually a sharp criticism of governmental power. The next words, "For there is no authority except from God," do not mean that government comes from God, but rather that the *power,* the authority which the government represents, is established by God. The authority that is inherent in the power to rule comes from God, for God, as John of Patmos never tires of reminding us, is the "King of kings," the "Ruler of the kings of the earth."

This point raises two critically important issues. First of all, it means that a government has power and authority *because, and only as long as,* it reflects the power and authority of God. Second, this authority is given by God, which the government must recognize. In Revelation 13 this fact is surrounded by tension. On the one hand, the dragon gives his power and his throne and his great authority to the beast. On the other hand, it is said that the beast from the sea was allowed to exercise authority, to make war, to work great signs. The issue is this: the beast is so clearly the "child" of the dragon that it receives its power from the dragon. Its power is so evil that it can come only from the dragon. At the same time this happens because God *allows* it to happen. John echoes here the faith of Israel articulated by Daniel: "You, O LORD, appoint kings; and you dethrone them" (see Dan. 2:21).

To know that is to know at once the nature and the limits of governmental authority. This was also the whole point of kingship in Israel. A king was king because, and only as long as, he represented the presence of Yahweh among the people. Kingship in Israel was authentic only inasmuch as it reflected the authority and power of Yahweh. That power is a shared, liberating, just, humanizing power, not for its own sake but for the sake of God's people —especially the poor and the oppressed.

Therefore, for the prophets as well as for the people of Israel, the criterion for true kingship was not military might, diplomatic victories, or the accumulation of wealth but rather the way in which the image of Yahweh was seen in the rule of the king. Israel understood from the very beginning that God's power was a creative power, making room for people to live in freedom and harmony with each other and the rest of creation. Moreover, the power of Yahweh to create was not kept by Yahweh alone but shared with human beings, so that they became co-creators with God.

The power of Yahweh is evident most of all in the liberation of Israel from the oppression of Egypt. In the exodus God uses this power to save the people from slavery, oppression, death, and destruction; for freedom, full humanity, and the joy of the service of the Living One. The people of Israel have experienced Yahweh's power in his sensitivity to their cries of pain and suffering *and* in the ten plagues, in the exodus *as well as* in the closing of the waters of the Red Sea. Indeed, they know Yahweh to be the One who will defend the afflicted and the oppressed. This God raises up prophets to defend the poor and the needy; this God takes up the cause of the orphan, the widow, and the stranger and pours wrath upon those who do injustice. This God has taught that true kingly rule does not lie in splendour but in doing justice. In the words of Jeremiah to king Jehoiakim (Jer. 22:13, 15–16):

> Woe to him who builds his house by unrighteousness
>   and his upper rooms by injustice.
> . . . .
> Do you think you are a king
>   because you compete in cedar?
> Did not your father eat and drink
>   and do justice and righteousness?

Then it was well with him.
He judged the cause of the poor and needy;
     then it was well.
Is this not to know me?
     says the LORD.

The power of Israel's God is a power that sets the prisoners free, upholds the cause of the oppressed, and gives food to the hungry. God uses this power to give sight to the blind, to lift up those who are bowed down, to sustain the orphan and widow, and to frustrate the ways of the wicked (Psalm 146).

Such is Yahweh, the King of kings. Such must be the kings of Israel and all those who have power and authority, for that power and authority come from God. No wonder Ezekiel speaks of the rulers of Israel as "shepherds" of God's people. It was their expectation that the ruler reflect the rule of God, that the ruler be a shepherd of the people who would, in the words of Ezekiel, bind up the crippled, feed the hungry, seek the strayed, strengthen the weak (Ezekiel 34). No wonder, too, that Paul the Jew, who knew scripture so well, would reflect that expectation in his view and understanding of civil government.

Some people say Paul could describe government so positively in Romans 13 because he wrote at a time when Nero was not yet the tyrant he later became. But Paul knew of the martyrs in Maccabean times who became victims of a demonized governmental power. He surely knew of the suffering of the Jews under successive Roman governments. He knew how easy it is for governments to condemn the innocent and to abuse their power.

What shaped Paul's thinking on the matter of civil government, I believe, was not his experience with an unusually friendly Roman government but his understanding of what government ought to be, as this understanding was given substance by the teaching of scripture. For this reason Paul begins with the affirmation that all authority comes from God. For this reason he continues to say "submit yourselves" and repeatedly makes the telling, significant point that government is no less than "God's servant for your good," while the language he uses here is not that of politics but of the liturgy! And it is for this reason that John meticulously makes the point, as revealing as it is chilling, when he speaks about the power of the beast: "And to it the dragon gave his power and his throne and great authority." The parody is clear, the inversion is complete, and the results are frightening.

Paul, in Romans 13, is at pains to make clear that it is expected of government to be an agent of God, a servant of God "for your good." The government is there for the good of the subject, even more precisely from a Christian point of view—which is also the whole point of tension in Romans 13—for the good of the neighbour. Also, good government, as the servant of God, knows and understands the difference between good and evil. Even the word "wrath" is understood to be a reflection of God's wrath against chaos, against the forces of evil, which resist God's purposes for justice, peace, wholeness, and human liberation. John's repeated statements about the blasphemies of the beast do not refer simply to what the beast *said*. They refer to the beast's actions, which are the complete opposite, the final denial, of the power, the actions, and the purposes of God.

Because governmental authority should be a servant of God for the good of God's people, it is inconceivable that a government can use the sword not to establish justice but to maintain injustice; not to secure liberation but to maintain slavery; not to break down but to maintain structures of oppression and inhumanity—and still be an agent of God. No. When this happens, this power becomes the beast from the sea. When government no longer distinguishes between good and evil, between what is humanizing and what is not, it is no longer the servant of God but the beast from the sea.

Demonic or demonized?

"[They] worshipped the dragon, for he had given his authority to the beast, and they worshipped the beast, saying, 'Who is like the beast, and who can fight against it?'" (13:4). Again the emphasis is that the beast has estranged itself completely from the Living One; its power is not an "authority given by God" but a demonized power conferred by the dragon, the devil, the liar, the deceiver. It is no wonder that people worship the dragon and the beast. They have been completely confused, deceived.

"And the beast was given a mouth uttering haughty and blasphemous words, . . . blaspheming [God's] name. . . . Also it was allowed to make war on the saints and to conquer them" (13:5–7). John is not saying that the power of the state as such is demonic. He is saying, however, that when the state denies that its power comes from God, and when it refuses to reflect God's serving, liberating, humanizing power, it no longer understands good and evil and no longer serves God or the people. Then what should have been a servant of God becomes a servant of the dragon. John is also saying, Beware and prepare yourself; it can happen, it *is* happening.

In South Africa, John's warning has become chilling reality. The state of affairs even at this time in our history is painfully clear—the continued racism, exploitation, and oppression; the continued inhumanity of the system; the incredible violence of the state and the ongoing terrorizing of the innocent. Our children are shot in the streets like dogs; our pregnant women are beaten and kicked by laughing soldiers; the judicial system finds torturers not guilty and declares murdering policemen free from all blame even if the evidence is there for all to see. Those who struggle for justice, peace, and genuine reconciliation on the basis of their Christian faith are charged with treason and subversion, are banned and killed. Those who support apartheid, who abet the evildoers in their evil, are rewarded with money and power. The upholders of apart-

heid and oppression, the killers of children, sit in parliament and call themselves "servants of God." Their words
are arrogant and blasphemous, for their power is not from
the Living One, the God of Israel, but from the dragon,
the deceiver and liar.

No, in the minds of millions of oppressed people there is
no doubt: The South African government is neither just nor
legitimate. In its ongoing oppression and exploitation of
the people, in its wanton violence in order to maintain this
oppression, in its persistent disobedience to the Word of
God, this government can no longer claim to be the servant
of God. It has become the beast from the sea. Dietrich
Bonhoeffer was right when he warned the church in Germany, "Hitler has shown himself for what he is, and the
church ought to realize with whom it has to reckon."

"One of its heads seemed to have a mortal wound, but
its mortal wound was healed" (13:3). Most commentators
take this to be a reference to Nero. It is not necessary to
argue that John was writing at the time of Nero even if this
is true. Nero's suicide in 68 could have been regarded as
a "mortal wound" that healed because of the general be-
lief that Nero was not really dead but would return. It may
also be that John is taking the beast as the parody of God
to its utmost consequences. Jesus is portrayed as the Lamb
who was slain and yet lives. Here the beast has a head that
was wounded and yet lives. The determination of this
beast to be like God is frightening, and it does not end
here. As we shall see, the beast from the earth shall complete this parody and the process of inversion.

John ends this first part (13:10) with a curious sentence
he has borrowed from Jeremiah:

> If any one is to be taken captive,
>   to captivity he goes;
> if any one slays with the sword,
>   with the sword must he be slain.

Almost all commentators see in these words a call for "endurance," which means nonviolence and suffering for the

persecuted Christians. They take it to be an injunction
that holds true even today under all circumstances.

This is not the place for a full discussion of the issues of
violence and nonviolence. Suffice it to say that I certainly
find no justification in the biblical message for the use of
violence, and I understand fully the principled stand of
the very early church on this issue when, in its refusal to
participate in the emperor's military, it held on to the
now-famous phrase: "It is not lawful for me to fight." What
I do find disturbing is the appalling hypocrisy always displayed on this point by Western churches and white Christians in South Africa and again evident in their reading of
this passage. Quite apart from the question of whether
John was indeed laying down a law for all times and all
circumstances, I must say this: If this injunction is a condemnation of the use of violence, it is more than a condemnation of Christians in Latin America and South
Africa who have taken up the gun in their struggle for
liberation. It is as much condemnation of all violence
Christians are involved in, including the violence of the
"just war." It condemns Luther as much as Münzer, Bonhoeffer as much as Oliver Tambo. Again, I do not say that
their interpretation is necessarily wrong, but I do protest
against the simple, pietistic exegesis which prescribes nonviolence for one group of Christians while saying not a
word about the violence of those who have forgotten what
it means to be oppressed, and who in their own history
have never hesitated to take up arms. Besides, John's
words leave us with a vexing question. If Christians are not
permitted and not even expected to use the sword, to
whom is John speaking when he warns that "if any one
slays with the sword, with the sword must he be slain"?
Surely he must be speaking to those who in this passage
use the sword: namely, the dragon, the beast, and their
representatives. If they are to be slain by the sword, who
is to do that—God? And, if so, how will he do it? Those who
do it will be doing the bidding of God. We cannot help but
think here of the "avengers from among God's servants,"

of whom Calvin spoke, who will remove the unjust rules. Will they stand condemned as well?

Apartheid is a Christian policy

The beast from the sea now gets a mate, the beast from the earth. "Then I saw another beast which rose out of the earth; it had two horns like a lamb and it spoke like a dragon. It exercises all the authority of the first beast in its presence" (13:11–12).

The description John gives is quite precise. It seems almost that he has someone specific in mind. He may well have, for the description fits the asiarch, the high priest of the imperial cult in the temple in Ephesus. The council of priests responsible for the imperial cult was a body with civil authority also. An idolized Caesar who had to be worshipped needed a temple, with priests and a liturgy. This he had, in Ephesus as well as in other places.

Some scholars believe that the high priest of the imperial cult also had the authority to issue coins on special occasions, which would account for John's imagery of the mark of the beast "on the hand." In any case, accepting the coins and using them is tantamount to accepting the idolized status of the emperor. There are others who believe that on special occasions the people received a real mark, which allowed them to participate in the festivities. The mark "proved" both their acceptance of the divine nature of the Caesar and their acceptability to the empire because of this. They would be safe, free from harassment and persecution. As slaves were branded to show that they were the property of their master, these worshippers were the property of the emperor—or, more properly, of the dragon.

One remembers the explanation of the Minister of Defence when the South African Defence Force, in their siege of Duduza township near Johannesburg, branded township residents on their hands with indelible ink. "It was to show," he explained, "that these people had already been interrogated and the army is now sure they are not involved in illegal activities. *It is a sign that they have nothing to fear.*" Many of us were puzzled, many stunned, many indignant. John of Patmos would not have been surprised at all.

John speaks about the second beast as it performs the liturgy of the blasphemous cult. "It works great signs, even making fire come down from heaven to earth" (v. 13); "it was allowed to give breath to the image of the beast so that the image of the beast should even speak" (v. 15); "it deceives those who dwell on earth" (v. 14). In its parody of Jesus Christ, this beast is doing precisely what Jesus in his life refused to do: tricks and wonders in order to deceive and, in deceiving, to persuade. It had to do what Jesus had no need for. But notice something else. John quietly insists that the second beast, like the first beast, was "allowed" to do certain things. Even with all their power, the two beasts are still ultimately under the power of the Living One. In the end, John says, these all-powerful beasts will have to acknowledge what the church already knows: Jesus Christ is Lord.

If the first beast is the demonized power of a corrupted and illegitimate state, who is the second beast? It is the religious or, if you will, the theological justification which the first beast absolutely cannot do without. This is the false prophet who provides the moral and theological justification for the work of the first beast. It has always been thus. Pharaoh did not himself become a priest; he had priests who proclaimed him god. In his power-hungry madness, Ahab did not abolish religion. He had no less than four hundred prophets attached to his court to assure him that what he was doing had the approval of God. It was only true prophets of God, such as Micaiah and Elijah, that he could not stand. Herod even had court theologians who explained to him the scriptures as they pertained to the birth of the Child. It was Christian Germany who elected Adolf Hitler, and it was Christians who shouted "Sieg Heil!" on the streets as well as from the pulpit.

In South Africa it is historically true that apartheid was

a church policy long before it became state policy; the Dutch Reformed Church proclaimed with pride in September 1948, "Apartheid is a church policy." This is the voice of the second beast, over the years articulating with increasing sophistication the theology of apartheid: from the Tower of Babel (the justification of the separation of people) to the words of Paul in Acts 17:26 (the justification of the homelands policy). This is the voice of the beast, which is quick to warn us when we plan a well-organized, peaceful march to demand the release of Nelson Mandela, telling us in a telegram released to the press that we should not resist the government. But when that same government attacks and kills the unarmed, defenceless marchers who responded to our call because they believe in nonviolent resistance rather than in revolutionary violence, those same churches say not a word.

It looks like a lamb, John warns, but it speaks like a dragon. It says peace! peace! where there is no peace. It speaks about reconciliation without the confrontation and the cost. This dragon which looks like a lamb is full of compassion for the anguish of the oppressor as he makes yet another "unavoidable" decision to kill the innocent. And yet it cannot hear the voice of God in the cries of the poor and the needy. It is the voice of those who believe that the sins of the church should be buried by history instead of confessed and forgiven. It is the voice of those who are so concerned about what may happen to white South Africans *one day,* after apartheid will have come to its inevitable end, that they show no concern at all about what is being done to black South Africans *right now.* It looks like a lamb, but its voice is the voice of a dragon. It is the voice that protests, even now, as the blood of our children stains the streets, "Apartheid is a Christian policy!" But the truth is out and cannot be suppressed: apartheid is not Christian, it is a blasphemy, an idolatry, and a heresy.

It is a human number

"This calls for wisdom: let him who has understanding reckon the number of the beast, for it is a human number, its number is six hundred and sixty-six" (13:18).

There has always been much ado about this, and there still is. Numerous and ingenious are the endeavours to find the solution to this problem, the answer to which, most believe, must be Nero. And indeed, the Hebrew numerical value of 666 is the name Nero, although it may also be the equivalent of the number 616. But why should John, while writing in Greek, all of a sudden pose a riddle in Hebrew? Is it not more logical that he would do this in Greek? But this cannot be done in Greek, for the Greek *Neron* yields a total not of 666 but of 1005. It can only be done in Greek if one accepts that the number is not 666 but in fact 616, which would be the total for *Nero.*

If one works on the basis of coins, however, as Ethelbert Stauffer does, the full Greek titles of Domitian, in abbreviated form, do add up to 666: Autokrator Domitianos Sebastos Germanicus. But then, of course, the answer is Domitian, not Nero. There is also another problem. There is no single coin on which all five titles appear together.

We believe that John intends a meaning that lies deeper than numerology. His wisdom is not the cleverness of juggling with names and numbers. Besides, what precisely does it prove if the number 666 totals up to Nero or, for that matter, to Domitian? The issue here is not the identification of the beast but rather the *existence* of the beast. John is saying, Look, his number is 666, three times it is almost 7, almost perfect. As we have said before, the parody is taken to its utmost consequences. It is a beast; it is a power. Yet it denies the true source of its power from God and receives it from the dragon. It is a beast, and although it looks like a lamb, it has the voice of a dragon.

John is also saying something else: "it is a human number." It is a human being. Don't be confused by the symbols as if they spiritualize the struggle, taking it out of our earthly history of sweat, blood, and tears into some eso-teric battle between the cosmic powers of good and evil. It is a human number—a human being abusing power that was given for the sake of good, overstepping the borders of what is permissible. In this way John reminds his read-ers that evil is not just a spiritual force. It has a human face.

At the beginning of our encounter with the beast, I made the point that John calls it beast because in it all humanity has been destroyed. As a result of its awesome powers, "the whole earth followed the beast with wonder" (13:3). It used its power to make war on the faithful and to wreak havoc and destruction. Out of fear and in their confusion, people worshipped the beast. They said, "Who is like the beast?" Even though they knew it was a beast and called it thus, they still worshipped it as if it were God. They completely forgot the testimony of Israel and the church: "None is like thee, O Lord." Now John says, Be wise, it is a human number. Yes, it is a beast, but it is human.

The poor and the oppressed have always understood this, and Desmond Tutu, bishop of God's oppressed people in Soweto and in South Africa, speaks for them all as he repeats John's truth to the face of Louis Le Grange, Minis-ter of Law and Order: "Mr Minister, you are not God. You are merely a man. And one day your name will only be a faint scribble on the pages of history while the name of Jesus Christ, the Lord of the church, lives forever."

6

The Fall of Babylon

Revelation 17–19

The end is coming, and it begins with the fall of Babylon. Actually the scene has already been set by chapters 15 and 16. Here the exodus is more firmly than ever the framework and inspiration of John's understanding of events. Rome is Egypt, as much the land of bondage and death as was Egypt in the story of Israel's liberation. Rome is visited with seven plagues, as complete and devastating as the ten that crippled Egypt. Now, as then, the plagues, one by one, challenge the power of Pharaoh, undermining his claims to omnipotence, exposing his powerlessness before the true God whose voice will now be heard and whose choice has been made clear. After the plagues comes the crossing of the sea while the pursuers are drowned like Pharaoh and his armies.

Then comes the "song of Moses" *and* the "song of the Lamb." This song is much more association than literal quotation. It is not the same song but it does convey the same message: The God of the exodus is the God of the church. The promises of the exodus holds also for the church in its struggle against this new Pharaoh. This is the true continuity of the biblical tradition: sharing not only the pain but also the promise; holding on not only to the memory but also to the vision; understanding the past but also shaping the future. That is why the exodus is the experience of Israel and the hope of the church; the song is the song of Moses and of the Lamb. It is the shared faith which gives understanding and knowledge to the church: We have seen this Pharaoh before, but the God of Israel is the same yesterday, today, forever. It is the unbroken promise which sustains: I am who I am; you will be my people, and I shall be your God.

"Who shall not fear and glorify thy name, O Lord?" (15:4). The question is purely rhetorical, filled with that secret, bubbling, yet contained joy of children posing a riddle the answer to which they already know. After all, the reason for the song is not slavery but liberation from slavery! In the end, Pharaoh had no choice: he had to let God's people go. In the end, Nebuchadnezzar had to bless "the Most high . . . who lives for ever; for his dominion is an everlasting dominion . . . and he does according to his will" (Dan. 4:34–35).

The question is put not in the quiet solitude of intellectual meditation but in the midst of the violent, fear-filled rage of oppressive and destructive forces, a question put not with trembling hesitation but with joyful certainty: "For thou alone art holy. . . . Thy judgments have been revealed" (15:4). The song of Moses was first sung on the other side of that sea. It was sung again in the words of Elisha to his servant as they saw themselves surrounded by the armies of an enemy king: "Fear not, for those who are with us are more than those who are with them" (2 Kings 6:16). It was sung again and again by the prophets and now again by the church. It is a song that praises God, not simply for the judgments on the enemies of God's people, but for the fact that these judgments and deeds are deeds of justice.

Chapter 16 is filled with plagues and anger, fear and curses. "The great city was split into three parts, and the cities of the nations fell. . . . Every island fled away, and no mountains were to be found" (16:19–20). There is lightning and thunder and a great earthquake. And yet this is not the end, it is only the beginning of the end. It is only the prelude to the final moments of Babylon.

The great harlot

John is transported to the desert to be shown "the judgment of the great harlot who is seated upon many waters" (17:1); "I saw a woman sitting on a scarlet beast" (17:3). We are again in the wilderness, and we are again faced with a woman. But this time the woman is the exact opposite of the woman we met in chapter 12. They are both women, they are both called "mother," but the differences cannot be more fundamental. In chapter 12 we met the Messianic mother, the giver of life. Here we are confronted with the mother of whores, the very personification of the evil she is associated with. She does not understand or give life. This woman is the mother of death, who does not nurture or protect but destroys. The Messianic mother brings forth a child who promises life to the world. The mother of death is "drunk with the blood of the saints and the blood of the martyrs of Jesus" (17:6).

The most striking thing about the great harlot is her intimate relationship with the beast. They belong together. The beast on which she sits is the same as in chapter 13, "full of blasphemous names, and it had seven heads and ten horns" (17:3). The woman is "bedecked with gold and jewels and pearls" (17:4). The obvious wealth has everything to do with the fact that she belongs to the beast; it is more than just the outward signs of her royalty. The point John wants to make goes deeper: the wealth Rome is so proud of is not a sign of God's blessing or Rome's hard work, it is directly related to the oppressive military might and economic exploitation that are the hallmarks of that society. The wealth of Roma Mater was built on the continued exploitation of weaker nations, on the robbing of the colonies, and on slave labour. It was the power of the beast that made possible the wealth of Rome. Then as now, John does not allow romantic notions about poverty and wealth to linger in the mind of the church.

Once more John returns to this theme in verse 15. "The waters that you saw, where the harlot is seated, are peoples and multitudes and nations and tongues." In verse 1 John notices that the great harlot "is seated upon many waters." It is very clear: the peoples and nations are under her feet; she sits upon them. The impression of oppression is inescapable. It is no wonder the woman and the beast are as one, at least for those who have eyes to see.

"When I saw her I marvelled greatly" (17:6), says John. There are some who connect John's astonishment to the wealth of the city. I cannot accept that. Oppressed people do not look in admiration on the riches of the oppressor when they know that those riches are the result of their own continued exploitation. Others, however, link John's astonishment to the "mystery of the woman," as the angel says in verse 7. That is indeed closer to the mark.

Usually it is understood thus: the "mystery of the woman, and of the beast," has to do with the identity of the seven heads and ten horns. This portion, so the argument goes, brings us closest to the identity of the emperor under whose reign the Apocalypse was written. The monster on whom the woman sits was and is not and is yet to be. This one, many say, is definitely Nero, who had committed suicide but was believed to be yet alive and in hiding, or dead, but who would return in any case. He is the one John refers to as the beast who will "ascend from the bottomless pit" (17:8). One lone commentator holds that the words "the beast . . . *is not*" are "the clearest possible indication that there was no open and organized persecution at the time when [John] was writing!" This I reject as pure conjecture, given the evidence in the Apocalypse itself and our knowledge of the background of both the times and the book. It is an effort to show at all costs that the Apocalypse, after all, is not a "revolutionary" but a "spiritual" book.

But to return. The seven heads are also seven kings, of whom the first five have fallen, one now is, and the other has not yet come; and when he comes his stay will be short. "As for the beast that was and is not, it is an eighth but it belongs to the seven, and it goes to perdition" (17:11). At first the matter looks relatively simple. All we need is a list of Roman emperors and we will be able to work out not only the riddle John is posing but also under whose reign he was writing. But it only seems simple. One can begin the list with Julius Caesar, and it will look as follows:

Julius Caesar died in 44 BC

Augustus reigned from 27 BC to AD 14

Tiberius reigned from AD 14 to 37

Caligula reigned from 37 to 41

Claudius reigned from 41 to 54

Nero reigned from 54 to 68

Then in one year follow the reigns of Galba, Otho, and Vitellius, which are considered by Suetonius as no more than rebellions, really, and not actually counted.

Vespasian reigned from 69 to 79

Titus reigned from 79 to 81

Domitian reigned from 81 to 96

If we start with Julius Caesar, the reigning emperor is Nero. If, however, we start with Augustus, as many do, then the reigning emperor at the time of John's writing is not Nero but Vespasian. But there are others who believe we should start counting with Caligula, since under his reign the crisis created by claims to imperial divinity and emperor worship began, even though he had no time to carry out his intentions. It is, then, not the chronological order of the emperors but the crisis of emperor worship which is the point of departure for the church.

But this line of argumentation presents many problems that cannot be resolved to the satisfaction of proponents on all sides. Who, they ask one another, is to decide where we are to begin counting? Why start with Julius Caesar and not with Augustus? But why with Augustus and not with Caligula? But then again, why argue about either

Julius or Augustus or Caligula and not at all about Tiberius? And why leave out Galba, Otho, and Vitellius? Those who believe that John wrote in the time of Nero cannot see Nero as the beast who "was and is not and is to come," although others argue that this beast from verse 8 is precisely Nero, and that John, like others of his times, expected that the myth of Nero returning from the dead would prove to be true. And if we start with Augustus and omit the three pretenders, then Vespasian is on the throne, Titus is the one whose reign will be short, since he "must remain only a little while" (v. 10), and Domitian is "an eighth [belonging] to the seven" (v. 11). He is then a second Nero, one as bad as Nero, reminding the church of the worst persecution it had undergone. But what then of the tradition preserved by Irenaeus that John wrote during the reign of Domitian? The answer is readily given: The very fact that John actually *knew* that the reign of Titus was short and that he calls attention especially to the eighth emperor pleads for dating the Apocalypse during the reign of Domitian, whom the church indeed did see as a second Nero.

All this has caused some commentators to end the confusion by taking a completely different tack. In the words of Martin Rist (p. 495):

> It is possible that none of these interesting conjectures is correct. In Daniel the four heads and the ten horns were used symbolically, not historically, and the same is true of the twelve eagle wings in II Esdras. Accordingly, it is conceivable that the beast had seven heads because of John's partiality for this number, or because in his sources there was a beast with seven heads, just as there was one with ten horns. One of the heads represents the present ruler, another the Antichrist who is to come; as for the other five, they may represent the imperial predecessors as a group, and not five specific individuals. Indeed, it has been suggested that John would probably have been unable to name the rulers of the century or more preceding the date of Revelation.

In the same vein George Caird says:

> The number seven is a symbol which John does not scruple
> to apply to earthly realities without insisting on numerical
> coincidence. . . . By the same token the seven kings are a
> symbolic number, representative of a whole series of emper-
> ors, and they would remain seven no matter how long the
> actual list happened to be.

But this same theologian says in the next line that "there
can be little doubt that the three heads are the three
Flavian emperors, Vespasian, Titus, and Domitian," inad-
vertently concurring with a critic who calls this argument
"very weak" exactly because John's choice of words makes
it clear that he was indeed thinking of individual emperors, not of some collective symbol.

I too have no doubt that John was referring to individual
emperors. I have no doubt that he was speaking of these
powerful men who had come and gone and done what
they had done to God's people through the years. Indeed,
he was grappling with a "mystery" as that mystery pertained to these powerful and violent men. But I believe
the scholars may have been looking for the wrong mystery. The mystery the angel seeks to make understandable
to John is not so much the identity of the man John is
speaking about. Surely he knew that, as did his parishion-
ers who read his letter. The mystery is not that the one
"who is and is not" is Domitian. I believe the mystery lies
in what happens to them rather than in who they are.

The key, therefore, lies in the words John repeatedly
uses to catch the attention of the church. "The beast
. . . was, and is not . . . and [goes] to perdition" (v. 8). And
again in verse 11, "As for the beast that was and is not, it
is an eighth . . . and it goes to perdition." The church
knows the beast. It has seen its power; it has suffered
immeasurably under its might. To the little people of God,
the powerless and defenceless *Christianoi*, the beast
seemed omnipotent. They have seen the whole world following the beast in admiration and wonder; time and time
again they have smelled its vile breath. But John says "the

beast that you saw"—in other words, the beast you know, the same one you have seen in action, whose wrath you have experienced—that same beast was and is not. Only the Messiah lives, the God whom we love and who loves us. He is and was and he shall come. Do not be misled, do not give up hope, the beast *is not,* he is already overcome, and therefore *he goes to perdition.* See, John says, others have come and they are gone, even Nero, whom the whole world, all those "whose names have not been written in the book of life" (17:8), thought would live forever. But we know better, we who belong to and believe in Jesus the Messiah. We know that in reality Nero is not, and he cannot rise from the dead; only Jesus can do that. And as for those who are still to come, the same fate is theirs; they shall not last, they go to perdition.

This is the background to that wonderful question in the song of Moses and the Lamb the church is singing as the prelude to the end of the beast and the harlot. "Who shall not fear and glorify thy name, O Lord?" (15:4). And the suffering church of Jesus the Messiah in South Africa understands. The political observers count tanks and missiles, soldiers and guns. They analyse the "strength" of Pretoria and count the threats and the dead bodies on the streets, and they smile paternalistically at the witness of the church. They ask us for the reasons for our "optimism." They do not understand the faith of the church, neither do they understand the continuity of the biblical tradition. When they see guns and more guns, they see power. The church sees a growing powerlessness: "it goes to perdition" (17:11). They scrutinize a new law that gives even more frightening powers to the Minister of Law and Order and to his "security forces." They see power. The church knows: "it goes to perdition." They look at the long lists of names of detainees, lists smuggled out of the country contrary to the laws of the state of emergency, and they see power. The church prays for those people, calls their names before the throne of God, and knows that "it goes to perdition," this beast. For the key here is not who the beast is; the church knows that. Neither is the key

whether we begin counting from D F Malan, or H F Ver-
woerd or P W Botha, from 1910 or from 1948. The key
here is the understanding of the mystery: this beast, this
powerful, merciless, violent beast, was and is not and goes
to perdition. "The beast that you saw was, and is not, and
is to ascend from the bottomless pit and go to perdition"
(17:8). It has no life and no future. It goes from hell to hell.

Once this is understood, the ten horns are no longer a
teaser in terms of identities. In that sense, they are no
longer interesting. John tells us something else. They are
kings of the earth over whom the harlot has great power
and authority. She has "dominion over them," even to the
extent that they wage war on her behalf against the Lamb.
First we hear that they are of "one mind" and willingly
give their power to the beast. They believe in the beast
and its power, and they accordingly share in the wealth
and power of the woman. But then something curious
happens. "And the ten horns that you saw, they and the
beast will hate the harlot" (17:16). They who have shared
her power and her favours, who have given over their
authority, now turn against her. Again and again John
hammers home the fact that the violence of the oppressor
shall be turned against him. Those on whom he depended
will desert him; indeed, shall seek his downfall. In the city
where the harlot had drunk the blood of the martyrs of
Jesus, "they will make her desolate and naked, and devour
her flesh" (17:16).

There is truth in the words we spoke to the apartheid
regime on 16 June 1986: Your life shall be like the life of
Ahab and the life of Jezebel. Your fate shall be the fate of
Babylon, which is called Egypt, which is called Rome,
which is called Pretoria.

But again, here we see the mystery John was told by the
angel. The kings of the earth turn against the harlot not
because they have so decided, neither because their political analysis has brought them to that point. No, they do so
because "God has put it into their hearts to carry out his
purpose" (17:17). Here then is the secret: Let the powerful
and the mighty, the princes and the potentates, make

their plans and plot their ways. In the end they will have to bow down to the will of the One whose purposes they will fulfil. Ultimately God, the King of kings, is in control. This is what John believes.

Let us speak once more of John's professed mystification as he stood there watching the woman and the beast. "When I saw her I marvelled greatly." He marvelled partly because of the mystery we have already spoken about. But there are some scholars who take this sentence to mean also that John was struck with admiration for the splendour that was Rome. I do not believe that at all. If there was any other reason for John's utter astonishment as he beheld the woman and the beast, it was the devastation of mind and feeling one experiences when confronted with the *mysterium iniquitatis* (2 Thess. 2:7). That is not so hard to understand. During the Second World War, even when what Nazism meant was no longer a secret, people were still shocked beyond words when they came upon a concentration camp or saw its victims; the actual existence of so much evil does take one's breath away. We know the feeling. Even now, knowing what we know about the South African "security forces" and what they do to black people during a state of emergency, when one suddenly is confronted with these killing machines in action, one cannot believe that human beings could actually do this to each other. I remember well my feeling when I saw the photographs of Steve Biko in September 1977, tortured to death by the South African security police—that young, vital, intelligent face, twisted beyond recognition, bereft of all humanity. That feeling is what John of Patmos must have experienced. "When I saw her I marvelled greatly." Indeed, this is the *mysterium iniquitatis.*

And just to make sure that there is no misunderstanding, that there would be no mistaking the identity of "Babylon the great, mother of harlots," John writes in verse 18: "And the woman that you saw is the great city which has dominion over the kings of the earth." She is still "great," she still has "dominion over the kings of the earth." Or so she thinks.

Cries of anguish, cries of joy

The whole of chapter 18 is the announcement of the destruction of Rome. The announcement is made by an angel with great authority, who brightens the earth with his splendour: "Fallen, fallen is Babylon." The judgment of God has come; what Rome has done to others she will now experience. Many commentators have seen the parallels with the prophecy of Nahum (3:1–5):

> Woe to the bloody city,
> all full of lies and booty—
>   no end to the plunder!
> The crack of whip, and rumble of wheel,
>   galloping horse and bounding chariot!
> Horsemen charging,
>   flashing sword and glittering spear,
> hosts of slain
>   heaps of corpses,
> dead bodies without end—
>   they stumble over the bodies!
> And all for the countless harlotries of the harlot,
>   graceful and of deadly charms,
> who betrays nations with her harlotries,
>   and peoples with her charms.
> Behold, I am against you,
>   says the LORD of hosts.

That last sentence is the clue: I am against you, says the Lord. With these words Nahum had also introduced this prophecy in 2:13, and this is what John has been saying from the beginning to the Nineveh of his day, Rome. The Lord is against you. God is against Rome, for God has chosen the side of poor, oppressed people. This was the discovery of Pharaoh, and Ahab, of Jezebel and Herod, of Nineveh and Rome—"I am against you." It was also the discovery of the faithless rulers of Israel who plundered and oppressed the poor and the destitute: "Thus says the Lord GOD, Behold, I am against the shepherds" (Ezek. 34:10). Israel knew, as the church knows: This is the most devastating of discoveries, that the Lord God, the Living One, is against you.

Of course one can try to ignore the meaning of this discovery, or one can try to hide inside the empty shell of what one calls power. Like Jezebel, reminding her husband of his power, "Are you not king of Israel?" (see 1 Kings 21:7). Or Rome: "Since in her heart she says, 'A queen I sit, I am no widow, mourning I shall never see' " (Rev. 18:7). Or P W Botha in his speech announcing the second state of emergency in one year: "South Africa stands alone in the world. But we have our security forces, our military might, our faith, and our God." They all make the same mistake. They depend on their arrogance and power, on their seemingly inexhaustible resources and their hold over others. After all, Rome "has dominion over the kings of the earth," she seduced the kings of the earth with her wealth and power, "and the merchants of the earth have grown rich with the wealth of her wantonness" (18:3). And when a South African ambassador boasts that the world, in its desire to put pressure on the South African government, should not forget South Africa's position as "superpower of the region," he forgets, like Rome, that the final indictment has already been delivered: "I am against you, says the LORD of hosts."

We must remember that as John writes there is no sign whatsoever of the imminent fall of Rome. He speaks like an Old Testament prophet. The vision is so clear, God's decision so certain, that for all intents and purposes it has already happened. Rome still stands, but already John can hear and see the rumblings and ripples of the mighty earthquake that will hit the city. He knows that the end of Rome is near. Rome still has "dominion" even as John writes, but, like Jesus, he has already seen Satan fall like lightning from heaven. Rome may still have power, but John knows we are seeing the beast's final convulsions.

Some scholars point to the differences in expectation here. According to chapter 6, the Parthians will attack and destroy Rome; chapter 17 creates the impression that some internal rebellion will finally cause the end of the empire. I do not believe it matters much. The point is, Rome is destroyed, the oppression is ended. In any case, it is God who has put it in their hearts. Human beings are mere instruments to fulfil the purposes of the Living One. And as Rome's destruction comes, the cries of those who have profitted from her power fill the air.

Who is weeping as Rome is destroyed? The kings of the earth, the merchants and the shipmasters. Those who were enriched through Rome's power, who with her exploited the poor and the weak. Those who captured her slaves and brought them to work for Rome's nobility in the same ships that brought the goods stolen from others. Notice John's sensitivity in his understanding of the workings of Rome's great economy. He gives us the lists of commodities brought to Rome by those same weeping shipmasters and merchants (18:11–13):

> And the merchants of the earth weep and mourn for her, since no one buys their cargo any more, cargo of gold and silver, jewels and pearls, fine linen, purple, silk and scarlet, all kinds of scented wood, all articles of ivory, all articles of costly wood, bronze, iron and marble, cinnamon, spice, incense, myrrh, frankincense, wine, oil, fine flour and wheat, cattle and sheep, horses and chariots, and slaves, that is, human souls.

Notice, first of all, how the slaves are put at the bottom of the list. They do not count; they are much less important than the splendid goods mentioned first. This is profound biblical criticism, completely in line with the fiery indignation of the prophets, of an economy where goods and profits are more important than people. What the Bible wants is an economy where people matter, where there is justice and equity.

But notice too how John corrects the thinking of a society where slaves did not count, or, even more pertinently, where there *were* slaves. He ends the list by mentioning "horses and chariots, and slaves, *that is, human souls.*"

Both slavery and racism require the fundamental dehumanization of the other in order to make the system work. At the basis of every such system, from slavery in the ancient world to apartheid in modern South Africa, lies the assumption, the absolutely necessary assumption, that the other is a non-person, somehow less than human. This is why that person's slave status, or inferior status, is justified. John of Patmos exposes and explodes this myth even as he exposes the system that makes it necessary. But slaves were cargo, and cargo was money. And now those merchants of goods and human flesh weep, for Rome is no more: "Alas! alas! thou great city, thou mighty city, Babylon!" (18:10). Rubbish, says John, the merchants cry because "no one buys their cargo any more" (18:11). The bottom line is not the splendour of Rome, it is money. The cries of anguish about the "investment climate" in South Africa today that emanate from London, Washington, and Bonn are not for the grandeur of this beautiful land or even for the suffering of the people. The bottom line now, as then, is money. How well John understood the nature of oppressors!

It is therefore slightly more than incongruous to read remarks of George Caird on this chapter of our book. He says (p. 227):

> The cry, "Was there ever a city like the great city?" is wrung from [John's] own heart as he contemplates the obliteration of the grandeur that was Rome. The proof of this is to be seen in the thoroughly material splendours of the holy city [*sic!*] into which the treasures and wealth of the nations are to be brought. There was nothing sinful about the commodities which made up Rome's luxury trade until the great whore used them to seduce mankind into utter materialism. . . . In the meantime it is with infinite pathos that John surveys the loss of *so much wealth.*

What shall we say of this view? Not much, except that it illustrates vividly the point that so much depends on where one stands in history as the struggles for freedom are waged across the world. It is so typically the viewpoint of those who do not know what it means to stand at the bottom of the list. No, the cries of the kings and merchants and shipmasters were *not* wrenched from John's own heart. Their cries were the cries of those who benefitted from oppression and got rich from exploitation—the captains and barons of industry, the privileged, the owners of Rome. The cry that found an echo in John's heart is the cry of the saints and apostles and prophets: "Rejoice over her, O heaven . . . for God has given judgment for you against her!" (18:20). It is the oppressed who rejoice, for their oppression will be no more. NO MORE! No less than five times more, John repeats these words. Babylon, the great harlot, the mighty and powerful, the oppressor and murderer of God's children, shall be *no more*.

O Lord, thou judge of all the earth

"After this I heard . . . the loud voice of a great multitude" (19:1). There is once again a song of praise and joy, which follows on the words of the angel at the end of chapter 18.

> Hallelujah! Salvation and glory and power
>   belong to our God,
> for his judgments are true and just.

The joy does not focus merely on the judgment as such but on the fact that God's judgments are just. But the church rejoices in the truth that God does avenge the blood of his servants.

"Then I saw heaven opened, and behold, a white horse!" (19:11). In Revelation 4, John sees a door that has been opened. This time, heaven itself opens. God sweeps aside a whole curtain to let John see everything there is to see. Nothing is withheld from his view.

What does he see, this banned pastor of the church? He sees the rider on the white horse, the Messiah making his triumphal entry. This time the Messiah does not come in the image of the lamb led without resistance to the slaughter. This time he will not stand mute before his accusers and be delivered into their hands. He comes as the rider

on the white horse. He has come to claim his reign, and
before him all pretenders to majesty and power, like the
idolatrous emperor, will be cowed and seen for what they
really are.

"His eyes are like a flame of fire" (19:12). John thinks of
the consuming fire from which Isaiah shrank back (Isa.
33:14); of the scorching flame Paul speaks about, which
will test all human works (1 Cor. 3:13). Nothing is concealed from the Lord. He uncovers—unmasks—everything. His eyes are a flame of fire—they burn with holy
wrath and the fury of God the Almighty. And ultimately
there is the sword, the sign of judgment and justice, that
comes from his mouth to strike the nations.

There is something that John cannot stop talking about
—the Lord's name. First we hear that his name is Faithful
and True. What kind of name is this? What other than *the*
name! The name he received after his victory over death
and the forces of hell, the name above all names. It is a
name that recalls *the* name: the echoes of the first announcement of the divine name sound clearly here—I am
what I am. Then, in those dark and terrible days of slavery
and bondage, of pain and death, Israel discovered the
firmness and truth of this name. He is what he is; he will
be what he will be. He will be there for his people, with
his people in the struggle with the Pharaoh, in the liberation from slavery, in the long, long trek through the desert. He was there. In the fiery words of the prophets, in the
condemnation of the powerful and the rich, in the protection and lifting up of the weak and the lowly, in the life
of Jesus of Nazareth. In all this he showed that he had the
power to do as he promised, to keep his covenant. So he
is called Faithful and True. John called him the faithful
Witness before, knowing that this Lord will do as he promised. Now he affirms that.

But we are not through with the richness of the meaning of this name. Presently John will say that only the rider
himself knows his name (19:12). But then John whispers
the name in our ears: he is called "The Word of God."
Eventually John will be able to contain himself no longer

and will sing it out jubilantly, his name is Lord of lords and King of kings.

Where are the lords who lord it over others, whose arrogance knows no bounds and whose "power" lies in violence and death, in threats and destruction? The one who conquered death and liberated men and women through his endless capacity to love, he is Lord of lords and King of kings. The time has come. Now every knee shall bow before him, and every tongue shall proclaim him Lord.

If his cloak is spattered with blood, it is the blood of his enemies, the destroyers of the earth and of his children. It is the blood of the tyrants who with immeasurable arrogance dare to challenge the *Kyrios*. And his judgment is terrible and final. The birds of prey are called to eat the flesh of those who have been struck down. It is the final sign that all life has ended, all is lost. "And the beast was captured, and with it the false prophet" (19:20). The two beasts who caused such havoc and destruction, so much pain and suffering, who misled and deceived the whole world—like Babylon, they are no more.

Once again an angel appears, holding the key to the bottomless pit, and into that same pit whence came the beast the serpent is thrown. Once again John mentions him by name, by *all* his names. Satan was conquered, and finally Death and Hades were conquered. One more time, one last time, there is fire and brimstone, death and destruction, until death itself dies. And then at last all is quiet, the earth is still.

> O Lord, thou Judge of all the earth,
> To whom all vengeance doth belong,
> Arise and show thy glory forth,
> Requite the proud, condemn the wrong.
>
> How long, O Lord, in boastful pride
> Shall wicked men triumphant stand?
> How long shall they afflict thy saints
> And devastate thy chosen land?

Our God, the refuge of his saints,
Will fight against iniquity;
Avenger of the innocent
The Lord omnipotent will be.

—James Malley, Psalm 94
from *The Psalter*, 1912

7

The End and the Beginning

Revelation 21–22

This is the closing drama. After the dragons and ser-
pents, battles and wars, after the death and destruction,
the waters are calm again. "Then I saw a new heaven and
a new earth; for the first heaven and the first earth had
passed away" (21:1). John makes clear that this is not a
return to some "paradise lost"; everything is new. Nothing
in heaven or on earth shall remind us of what has been.
And the sea—that abode of the unforeseen and the unpre-
pared-for, that source of evil and threat, that ever-restless
monster prowling along the shores of our lives—that sea
is no more.

A new heaven and a new earth

There must be a new earth. This earth, raped, robbed,
torn, filled with anger and revenge, with hurt and pain,
cannot and should not remain. It has to go. This earth had
been the dwelling place of the beast, the false prophet of
the beast who came out of the sea. It was the throne of
Babylon, the great harlot. This earth had given refuge to
the murderers of the saints of God but became, by the
same token, the arena of the suffering and death of God's
children. It was never "home" for them. On this earth
they were captured, made slaves, suffered for their faith.
This is the earth that soaked up their blood as it had drunk
the blood of those who had gone before them: Abel, Na-

both, the prophets, Jesus. It was not for nothing John so often used the phrase "the kings of the earth." Indeed, in the experience of the little people of God, the earth belonged to the mighty and the powerful who claimed it for themselves, and they were the enemies, the killers of those who sought to remain faithful to Jesus Christ. So this earth should be no more.

That we understand, but a new heaven? Are the heavens not the dwelling place of the Living One? Yes indeed, but in this age of painful contradiction, of not fully understanding, of looking into a mirror darkly, the ancient easterner knew: in that same heaven the dragon appears. In that same heaven he takes up his position to do battle with God for total possession of the earth and of those who call themselves God's children. That same heaven does not prove to be enough protection for the Messianic Mother as she faces the awesome power of the dragon. But there is more: there has been so much death and pain and suffering that the cries of God's children have choked up the skies. And not only God's children, indeed, "the whole creation has been groaning in travail together until now" (Rom. 8:22). The flames of the dragon's breath have polluted heaven's beauty; it is no longer sanctuary or sanctified.

How well should we understand this, we people of the twentieth century. We saw the heavens polluted by the foul and vile smoke from the factories, made hopelessly inhabitable for the birds of the sky in the name of progress. We know about "missiles carving highways of death through the stratosphere," as Martin Luther King said, and we understand fully Dorothee Sölle's fearful anger when she speaks about nuclear weapons being an attack on the life of God himself. Can the heavens ever be clean again after Hiroshima and Nagasaki? Can the heavens ever be purified of the stench of gas ovens, burnt-out villages in Asia, or utterly destroyed Palestinian camps in Lebanon? And of the vilest stench of all: those powerful and mighty men in top hats, sashes, and uniforms who threaten and maim, kill and destroy, and then go to prayer

breakfast and call upon the name of God: *"Gott mit uns,"*
"In God We Trust," *"Soli Deo Gloria."* No, John is so right
—there must be a new earth *and* a new heaven.

The vision of a new heaven and a new earth, comes, like
so much else in this book, from the Old Testament. It is
Isaiah's vision (Isa. 65:17–25). It is a radical transformation
of the heavens and of the earth; nay, more, a totally new
creation God has in mind. It is a vision in which the dream
of God is realized for those whom he loves:

> For behold, I create new heavens and a new earth;
> and the former things shall not be remembered
>   or come into mind.
> But be glad and rejoice for ever
>   in that which I create;
> for behold, I create Jerusalem a rejoicing,
>   and her people a joy.
> I will rejoice in Jerusalem,
>   and be glad in my people;
> no more shall be heard in it the sound of weeping
>   and the cry of distress.
> No more shall there be in it
>   an infant that lives but a few days,
>   or an old man who does not fill out his days,
> for the child shall die a hundred years old,
>   and the sinner a hundred years old shall be accursed.
> They shall build houses and inhabit them;
>   they shall plant vineyards and eat their fruit.
> They shall not build and another inhabit;
>   they shall not plant and another eat;
> for like the days of a tree shall the days of my people be,
>   and my chosen shall long enjoy the work of their hands.
> They shall not labour in vain,
>   or bear children for calamity;
> for they shall be the offspring of the blessed of the LORD
>   and their children with them.
> Before they call I will answer,
>   while they are yet speaking I will hear.
> The wolf and the lamb shall feed together,
>   the lion shall eat straw like the ox;
>   and dust shall be the serpent's food.
> They shall not hurt or destroy

in all my holy mountain,
says the LORD.

Isaiah's imagery is profoundly earthly, and such is also
John's intention. There is no reason for us to believe that
John is intentionally transporting Isaiah's vision into another world to come. The concern of the Apocalypse is not
so much the creation of another world (a "next world")
into which the church is called to escape. The whole point
of John's writing is that it is in *this* world, in this human
history, that the power of the Lord will be seen. It is for
this reason that the triumphant church is not transported
into the new Jerusalem, transported into the next world,
but that the new Jerusalem comes down *out of heaven.*

We need not see this as an occasion to argue about the
question of "eternal life." John does not deny it. He believes simply that it begins now. The dream of God, which
is the vision of Isaiah and of John, does not wait for "eternity" but is being realized where the cold inhuman reality
of history is met and overturned by the warm, humanizing
reality of the dream of God. The new Jerusalem is not an
unreal mirage from beyond; it is a city that arises on the
ashes of Babylon, which is now being destroyed. Put differently, this city—where we shall enjoy our labour and our
children, where our children shall live to bear children
and not die untimely, where we shall build homes and live
in them without fear of being driven out by war or influx
control or the Group Areas Act, where there shall be
peace so that no one will "hurt or destroy," where we shall
actually hear the voice of the Lord even before we call—
this city need not wait for the new Jerusalem but can arise
on the ashes of all that "Pretoria" stands for now, for the
old things have passed away.

The tent of God

A great voice thunders from the throne, saying, "Behold, the dwelling of God is with the people" (21:3). It is
not an angel who speaks; this announcement is far too

important. The great voice comes from the throne. Maybe
it is God who speaks, but John cannot yet bring himself to
say it out loud. The feeling persists, however, that we have
arrived at a momentous occasion—as indeed we have. The
"dwelling of God" is a reminder of the tent of God that the
people of Israel took with them at the exodus. As they
trekked through the wilderness, that tent was pitched in
the camp, a symbol and reminder of the presence of God
among them. As the people of Israel left Egypt, they knew
not where the road would lead. There was no blueprint,
no fully worked-out strategy, no certainty about the future. Israel had only the voice, that voice which gave a
promise of God that God would bring them to the promised land. Israel had no certainty; the only certainty was
the presence of God symbolized by the tent of God. The
presence of God became the embodiment of the voice,
and the certainty of fulfilment. It is a reminder also of the
blessing of Leviticus 26:12: "And I will walk among you,
and will be your God, and you shall be my people."

Some scholars point out that since there is no temple in
the new Jerusalem, John cannot be taken literally on this
point. They are right, of course. What John means is this:
For the first time that blessing has actually come true. God
has pitched a tent amongst the people, for God feels at
home with them. God's time amongst the people has
come, and this renewed world is such that God can feel at
home there.

I think I understand John. The God who longs to teach
the nations how to "beat their swords into plough shares,
and their spears into pruning hooks," cannot be at home
in a land "filled with horses, [where] there is no end to
their chariots" (Isa. 2:4, 7). A God who passionately wants
the nations to stop learning war can never be at home in
a world where livings are made from war and destruction,
where those who murder children made in God's own
image are decorated, and where violence and death are
glorified. A God who wishes fervently that the people
would understand what it means to walk in the light of the
Lord cannot be at home in a world whose people have

filled their land with idols, where they bow down to the work of their hands and to what their fingers have made. A God who has made human beings in God's own image cannot be at home in a world where these human beings are humbled and brought low. Indeed, a God who has made heaven and earth, looked at the finished work, and seen that it was very good, cannot be at home in a world where there are, in poet Cecil Rajendra's words,

> ruttish bulldozers
> debauching virgin forests.

A world where little children die untimely because they eat shreds of newspaper mixed with scraps of food, like the desolate children of South Africa's relocation camps—no, such a world cannot be home to the God of the exodus, of the prophets, of Jesus of Nazareth. It simply cannot be called home for the children of God's heart.

John longs passionately for another day, another world. He feels it so keenly that he says, with full conviction: That day has come. The church shares this longing, for the tent of God to be amongst the people. This is what the church has lived and died for, worked and struggled for: justice and humanity and peace and fulness of life. We can taste it already, and we rejoice in the day when we shall share the full meal of the Lamb. This is the longing expressed in the fervent prayer "Come, Lord Jesus." Be at home with us.

"And he who sat upon the throne said"—if John could not say so before, he now knows with certainty: it is God who speaks; for the first time in the Apocalypse, the voice John hears is the very voice of God: " 'Behold, I make all things new' " (21:5). It is Yahweh who is doing all this. John knows as well as we do that our new ideas and plans become old so quickly. "New" freedoms degenerate into slavery before we know it, and how often do we turn the joys of liberation into the desperation of a new tyranny. We seem cursed with the cynical wisdom of Ecclesiastes 1:9: "There is nothing new under the sun." Capitalism came to the world as the new guarantee of progress and development for all people. We would have prosperity hitherto unknown to humankind. Yet capitalism turned out to be a system that consistently benefits the privileged few, that cannot survive without constant exploitation of the poor, that thrives on our basest instincts. So what is new? Marxism promised the world freedom and equality, brotherhood and dignity. Yet how quickly has it become a system that fears freedom and regulates human dignity, and how depressingly oppressive has its main proponent proved itself to be in the world!

Even now the officials of the white Dutch Reformed Church in South Africa are trying to save apartheid from the rubbish heap where it has already been thrown and where it rightly belongs by claiming (once again!) that apartheid is not wrong because its intentions were so pure in the beginning.* It had in mind, they say, not injustice but justice, not oppression but freedom for all the different groups. But how quickly did the real nature of apartheid and those who defend it become visible! The ideological core of apartheid, racial separation in order to reserve "God-ordained" identities, was not new at all; we saw it in Hitler's Germany. No wonder that, as the apartheid state developed, more and more it took on the character of Hitler's Germany in its openly fascist mind, its growing militarism, its love of and dependence on violence, the mindless madness of its leaders, the cold-bloodedness of its managers, the violent and pitiful schizophrenia of its adherents, the total hopelessness of its future. "Behold," says God, creator of heaven and earth, protector of the innocent, helper of the poor and lowly, friend of the stranger and the homeless, lover of people, "I make all things new."

They who conquer shall have this heritage; they shall inherit all God has to offer in this new creation. In the seven letters to the seven churches, the promise is that the faithful, the conquerors, shall have *something:* the hidden

---

Editor's Note: In October 1986 the Dutch Reformed Church declared that apartheid is not a biblical imperative and cannot be scripturally justified.

manna, a new name, power over the nations, white gar-
ments, a seat on God's throne. But now God's generosity
knows no bounds. The conqueror receives all. And with a
loving gentleness that is almost too precious, too fragile to
leave in human hands, "And I will be his God and he shall
be my son" (21:7). No announcement to the masses here,
no thunder and lightning for all to see and hear, but a
tender whisper meant for one heart only—A quiet word
from God, light as a flower's sigh upon a single soul.

But immediately, almost rudely, John brings us back to
the reality of the situation. Those who are thus spoken to
receive this reward for their faithfulness, their willingness
to suffer for the cause of Christ. "But as for the cowardly,
the faithless, the polluted, as for murderers, fornicators,
sorcerers, idolaters, and all liars, their lot shall be in the
lake that burns with fire and brimstone, which is the second death" (21:8). We are taken by surprise. Almost
against our will, we are reminded of those grim moments
two chapters ago. But John is relentless. There is a struggle
going on, he reminds the church. There is a fight to fight,
and what counts now is the endurance of the saints, faithfulness, willingness to take upon ourselves the awesome
risks of discipleship. Being part of the body of Christ is not
only singing or speaking. It is also risking one's life for the
sake of truth. It is no wonder, then, that this list of the
accursed is headed by the cowardly and the faithless.

People who have never been persecuted for their faith
or vilified, smeared, and imprisoned because of their testimony for Jesus Christ will have great difficulty understanding these words of John. This is not the usual list of
"sinners" in the moral sense, as we might find with Paul.
Every category John mentions is connected with the
struggle of the church and the witness of the church
against emperor worship. "Murderers" here are not sim
ply those who take another's life but are especially those
who have killed the saints who refuse to participate in the
worship of the idolized Caesar. By the same token, "fornicators" here may well mean those who are seduced by
other gods, in this case the Caesar who calls himself "god,"

in the same way that the kings and powerful of the earth "fornicated" with Rome, the great harlot who had seduced them with her sensuous beauty. "Sorcerers" are those who beguile others so that they would participate in worshipping the god-man in Rome, in the same way that the beast of the earth beguiled the whole world to worship the beast from the sea. All these belong with death and will go where Death and Hades went: the lake of fire and brimstone.

Once more, only those who understand the painful price of discipleship will understand what John is saying here, and why the lot of cowards and the faithless is so different from the lot of those who remain faithful. In any case, this was well and truly understood by the writer of the Belgic Confession, Guido de Brés, who, knowing that he too will have to pay the price for holding on to the vision of Isaiah and John of Patmos and Jesus, wrote these immortal lines:

> The faithful and elect shall be crowned with glory and honour; and the Son of God will confess their names before God his Father and his elect angels; all tears shall be wiped from their eyes; and their cause, which is now condemned by many judges and magistrates as heretical and impious, will then be known to be the cause of the Son of God. . . . Therefore we expect that great day with a most ardent desire, to the end that we may fully enjoy the promises of God in Christ Jesus our Lord.

Fittingly, de Brés ends with the prayer from the heart of John of Patmos: "Amen. Come, Lord Jesus!" But in the words of the old black spiritual, in order to understand this fully, you had to be "there, when they crucified my Lord."

The bride of the Lamb

Again the scene changes drastically, and once again it is an angel who speaks. "Come, I will show you the Bride, the wife of the Lamb" (21:9). Once before John has spoken of the marriage feast of the Lamb, but the identity of the bride was not disclosed. Who can she be, the Bride of the Lamb? John is in for a surprise. The Bride of the Lamb is not, as one may expect, the 144,000 elect ones, the perfect number indicating those who are saved, representing the totality of the tribes of Israel. She is not the angels, or the saints who have suffered so for the sake of the Lamb. The Bride is not the church but the world, the holy city. There are those who have noted the parallels in the description of this holy city with the descriptions of the actual ancient city of Babylon, though what John's meaning could be remains unclear. However, the city may well represent the world. Ultimately, God's concern is not simply a pure church but a purified world, a new creation. I am once again astonished at the number of pages commentators use to come to grips with this vision (even to the point of trying to work out why the measurements don't really add up!), only to come to such conclusions as "a city shaped like a cube, with such extraordinary dimensions—1500 miles each way—is difficult, if not impossible to conceive." But that is exactly John's point. For the city is not a city but stands for the world, God's world in which God's permanent presence is the sign of God's blessing and at-homeness. It is also the sign of the world's redemption; it has passed from the hands of the mighty and the powerful into the hands of the One to whom it truly belongs. No wonder its description is really beyond all description. Twice John marvels: "And the city has no need of sun or moon to shine upon it, for the glory of God is its light, and its lamp is the Lamb" (21:23). And again: "They need no light or lamp or sun, for the Lord God will be their light" (22:5). John marvels, for at last it is seen and acknowledged by all that Jesus Christ is indeed the light of the world. The darkness has not overcome it, can never again overcome it. In this city God's servants will worship him, John writes.

What some today may take as a statement of the obvious was for John a wonder of God's grace: "His servants shall worship him" (22:3). Gone is the fear of persecution and death. Gone are anxious moments, the moments of pain and suffering. Gone also are the struggle and the need to die for what is right. "Normal" is no longer hiding in the night, leaving loved ones behind and fighting with wild beasts for the enjoyment of the Beast. What is normal now is walking in the light of God and living from the fruits of the tree of life. Over against the sixfold "no more" of Babylon after her destruction stand the sevenfold "no more" of God's city of delight and peace. Crying shall be no more; death shall be no more; mourning shall be no more; pain shall be no more; the sea shall be no more; neither night nor darkness. For God so loved the world.

The final divide

"These words are trustworthy and true" (22:6). Over against the preposterous claims of the liar, the deceit and propaganda of the emperor, is the word of the God who cannot lie. The "power" of the Caesar stands exposed as pseudo-power, which cannot stand the test of truth. In the Apocalypse, as well as in the Johannine writings, God is seen as the personification of truth. The lie is therefore not to be understood as a word that does not correspond with the actual facts, at least not primarily, but must be seen as the existence and actions of the forces which agitate against the will, the truth of God. As God is the personification of truth, so the idolized emperor becomes the personification of untruth. His words are lies because his actions contradict the presence and the will of God. God's words, however, as John never tires to remind us, are faithful and true and trustworthy.

> And he said to me, "Do not seal up the words of the prophecy of this book, for the time is near. Let the evildoer still do evil, and the filthy still be filthy, and the righteous still do right, and the holy still be holy. Behold, I am coming soon, bringing my recompense" (Rev. 22:10–12).

This is the last judgment, the final divide. John's language is so quiet, so sober, that it scares us to death. And so it should. It means simply, irrevocably, that God's mercy comes to an end. They have heard, they know, now it is over. This is the terrible equalization: What has been said of the Pharaoh and has been said of the Caesar is now being said of those who have ears but refused to hear, eyes but refused to see. So there is a tragic, mad persistence in their doing of evil. The same tragedy befell the Pharaoh when he hardened his heart. He had heard the voice of Moses, he had seen the effect of the plague. Why would he not hear and understand? Why indeed? Why cannot white South Africa listen and be saved by letting our people go? Why ask for more money for a "defence budget" when there is no defence against the wrath of God? Why continue with deceitful propaganda on radio and television and in newspapers when the truth is bound to come out? Why indeed? Political observers repeat the wisdom Rome was taught through its own history: "Those whom the gods wish to destroy, they first make mad." The church merely echoes John of Patmos: "Let the evildoer still do evil, and the filthy still be filthy." But let the righteous continue to do what is right and the holy still be holy. The great divide, the *final* divide, is here.

The bright morning star

There is still one more thing. Stauffer tells us that the court poet Martial had written a poem for Domitian, praying for the emperor's return from the north.

> Thou, morning star,
> Bring on the day!
> Come and expel our fears,
> Rome begs that Caesar
> may soon appear.

The church smiles at this last desperate attempt at power and glory. It has heard all too clearly the words of its Lord: "I am the Alpha and the Omega, the first and the last, the beginning and the end. . . . I am the root and the offspring of David, the bright morning star" (22:13, 16). Like death and darkness, like tears and crying and night, lies have come to an end. The Caesar may still convince himself, he may even mislead those who follow him, but the church knows better. God's truth will live forever.

What is left as John surveys God's city of justice and peace, the city of delight and light, is the longing of the church: Come, Lord Jesus.

For the pain and the tears and the anguish must end. . . . Come, Lord Jesus.

For the comfort of this world is no comfort at all. . . . Come, Lord Jesus.

For there must be an end to the struggle when the unnecessary dying is over. . . . Come, Lord Jesus.

For the patterns of this world must change. . . . Come, Lord Jesus.

For hate must turn to love; fear must turn to joy. . . . Come, Lord Jesus.

For war must cease and peace must reign. . . . Come, Lord Jesus.

The Spirit and the Bride say "Come." And let them who hear say "Come."

It ends as it began. But now the saints *know* what it means. "The grace of the Lord Jesus be with all the saints. Amen."

Selected Bibliography

Aalders, G J D. *De Grote Vergissing.* Kampen, no date.
———. *Van Huisgemeente Tot Wereldkerk, De Eerste Drie Eeuwen Christendom.* Kampen, no date.
Baumeister, Theofried. *Die Anfänge Der Theologie Des Martyriums.* Münster, 1979.
Baus, Karl. *History of the Church. Volume I, From the Apostolic Community to Constantine.* New York, 1980.
Bettenson, Henry S., ed. *Documents of the Christian Church,* 2nd ed. Toronto, 1963.
Betz, Hans D. *The Tyrant in Apocalyptic Literature.* Unpublished paper, 1980.
Boesak, Allan A., and Charles Villa-Vicencio, eds. *When Prayer Makes News.* Philadelphia, 1986. *A Call for an End to Unjust Rule.* Edinburgh, 1986.
Caird, George B. *A Commentary on the Revelation of St John the Divine.* New York and London, 1966.
Charles, Robert H. *Critical and Exegetical Commentary on the Revelation of St John.* Edinburgh, 1920.
Cunningham, Angus. *The Early Church and the State.* Philadelphia, 1982.
Davies, J G. *The Early Christian Church: A History of Its First Five Centuries.* Grand Rapids, 1981.
Ford, J Massyngberde. *Revelation* (Anchor Bible, vol. 38). Garden City, N.Y., 1975.
Frend, W H. *Martyrdom and Persecution in the Early Church: A Study of Conflict from the Maccabees to Donatus.* Grand Rapids, 1981.

Glasson, T Francis. *The Revelation of John* (The Cambridge Bible Commentary). Cambridge, 1965.

Grant, Robert M. *The Sword and the Cross.* New York, 1955.

Kroon, K H. *Openbaring I & II.* Verklaring Ven Een Bijbel-gedeelte. Kampen, no date.

Lenski, Richard C H. *The Interpretation of St John's Revelation.* Minneapolis, 1935.

Paton, Alan. *Ah, But Your Land Is Beautiful.* London, 1981; New York, 1982.

Rist, Martin. "Introduction" and "Exegesis" of "The Revelation of St. John the Divine," *Interpreter's Bible,* vol. 12. Nashville, 1957.

Roloff, Jürgen. *Die Offenbarung Des Johannes* (Zürcher Bibel-kommentare). Zürich, 1984.

Rowley, H H. *The Relevance of Apocalyptic: A Study of Jewish and Christian Apocalypses from Daniel to the Revelation,* 3rd rev. ed. Greenwood, S.C., 1980.

Russell, David S. *Apocalyptic: Ancient and Modern.* Philadelphia, 1968.

Stauffer, Ethelbert. *Christ and the Caesars.* Tr. by K. and R. Gregor Smith. London and Philadelphia, 1955.

Suetonius. *Lives of the Caesars* (Penguin English Translation). London, no date.

Van Hartingsveld, L. *Openbaring, Een Praktische Bijbelverklaring.* Kampen, 1984.

Visser, A J. *De Openbaring Van Johannes* (Prediking Van Het Nieuwe Testament). Nijkerk, 1972.